JASON WARD

CHILLING COCKTAILS

CLASSIC
COCKTAILS
WITH A
HORRIFYING
TWIST

THUNDER BAY
P · R · E · S · S
San Diego, California

INTRODUCING CHILLING COCKTAILS

It can be thrilling to watch a scary movie alone in the dark, but it's never quite as much fun as when you have company. Alongside comedy, horror is film's great communal genre. Whether it's an entire cinema jumping in unison at *Get Out* or a night in with some friends and a gory B-movie, a horror movie always feels like an event—and any good event deserves a decent drink.

Cocktails, with their high alcohol content, numerous ingredients, and complicated preparation techniques, are special drinks for special occasions; perhaps if beer came with a little umbrella or a sparkler every now and then we might think of it the same way too, but it doesn't.

The cocktails and party snacks in this book are inspired by some of the most significant horror films and books ever made and written; even though that inspiration is sometimes little more than an outrageous pun—think of it as being like those '90s movie sound tracks which included songs "inspired by the film."

These drinks make an excellent accompaniment for a film viewing (it's admittedly harder to down vodka cocktails while reading *The Turn of the Screw*) but they can be made anytime: and, of course, you don't actually have to watch *Let the Right One In* every time you fancy a Mai Tai.

Taking the time to create a special cocktail is a worthwhile endeavor, but the important thing to stress about these recipes is you're encouraged to mix things up out of taste or necessity. A brilliant rum cocktail, for instance, might also be a brilliant gin cocktail. If you haven't got any vermouth in the house, use sherry. If you don't like one type of juice, try another.

It's useful to think of cocktails not as an immutable concoction but as a balance of different elements—usually a spirit, something sweet, and something bitter or sour—and substitute, accordingly. Some of the most popular cocktails have arisen from this very process.

Many of these recipes suggest a garnish, but this is an aesthetic and strictly optional. That said: as Hannibal Lecter would undoubtedly tell you just before he flambéed your kidneys, aren't aesthetics the whole point?

BASIC BAR & COCKTAIL KIT

Collins glass

Highball glass

8

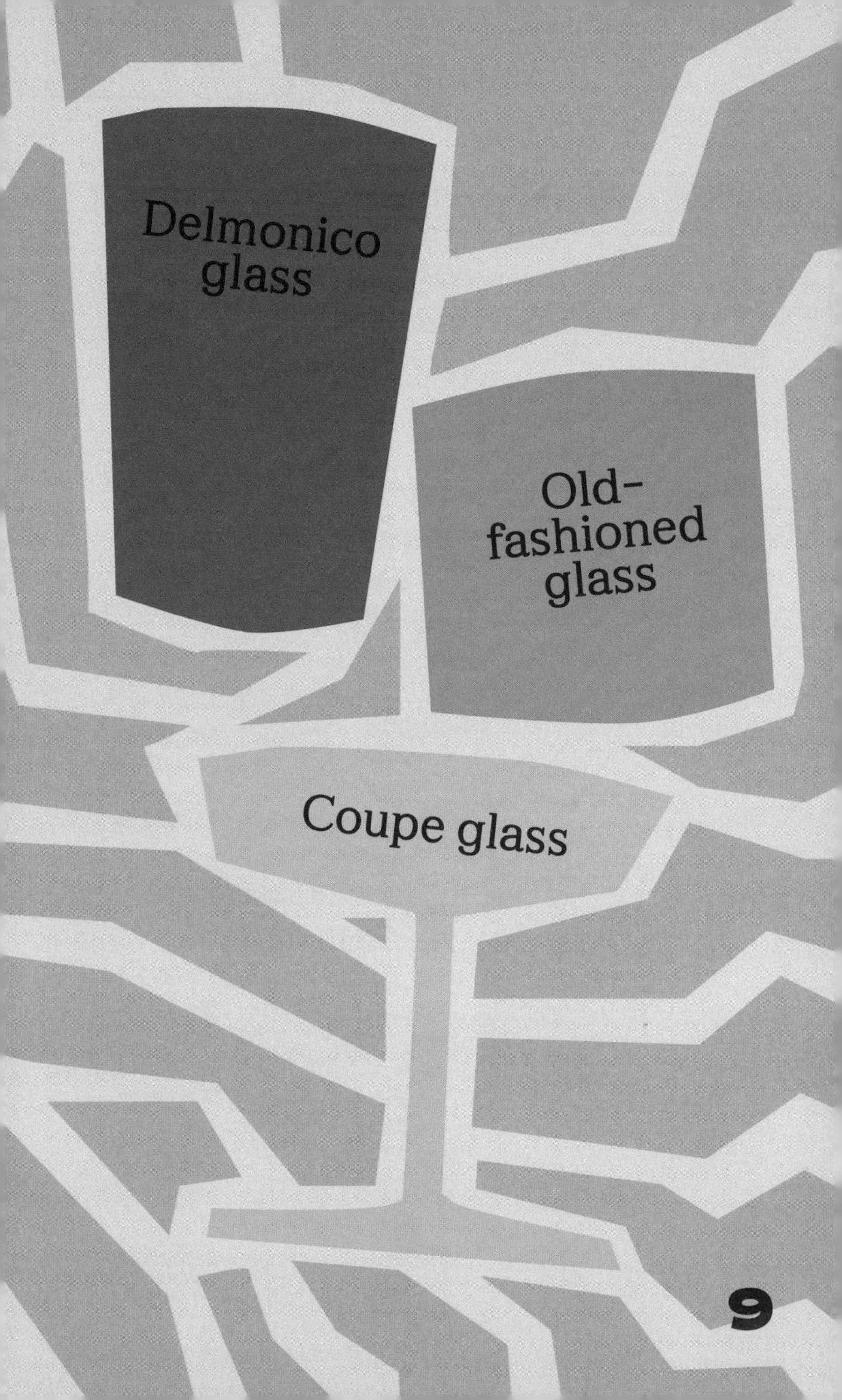

Delmonico
glass

Old-
fashioned
glass

Coupe glass

Martini
glass

Hurricane
glass

Shot
glass

10

Champagne
flute

Beer stein

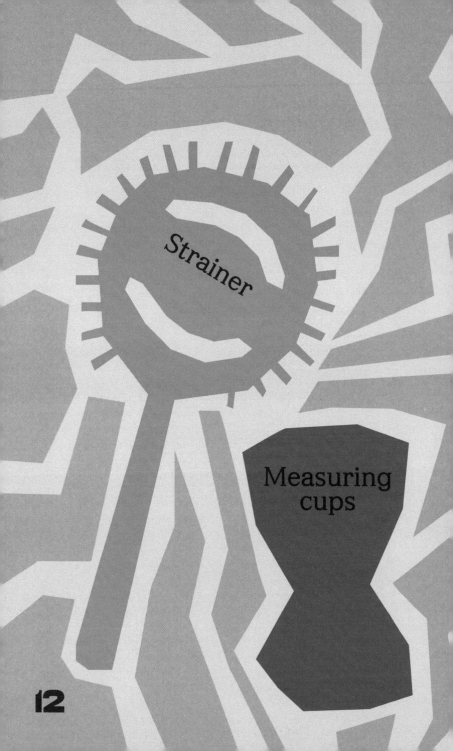

Strainer

Measuring cups

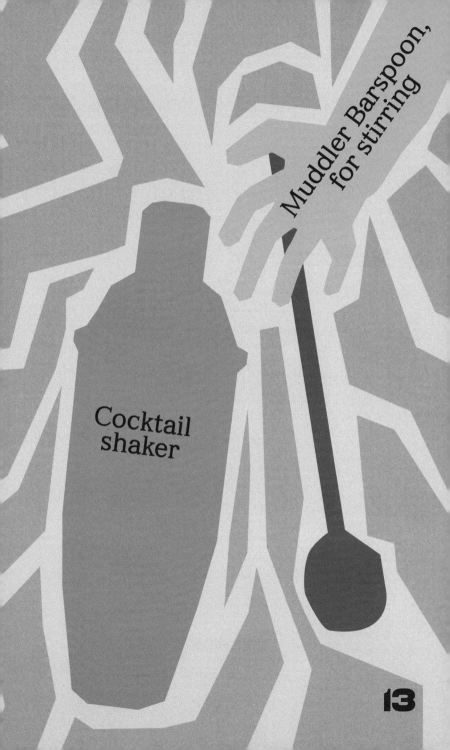

Muddler Barspoon, for stirring

Cocktail shaker

13

BASIC TECHNIQUES

Shaking

This mixes the ingredients, releasing their flavors and diluting the drink. Add the ingredients to a cocktail shaker filled with ice, tighten the lid and shake vigorously for at least 20 seconds until the shaker is cold and condensation has formed on the outside.

Stirring

Use a barspoon (a regular spoon is also fine) to make a circular motion for about a minute.

Straining

This prevents ice and solid ingredients from getting into the drink. You can use a dedicated strainer, although some cocktail shakers come with a strainer as part of the lid.

Muddling

Similar to shaking, crushing fruits and herbs allows them to release their flavor and infuses the drink. Using a sturdy glass, twist the muddler as if using a pestle and mortar.

Layering

Certain recipes (for instance From Dusk Tequila Dawn, page 62, and Candyman, Candyman, page 102) require layers of ingredients with different densities. Pour the required quantities over the back of a spoon.

Twisting

To extract the oils from the skin of a citrus fruit, take a piece and twist it over your drink. The twist can then be used as a garnish.

TABLE OF MEASURES

1 dash	12 drops
¹⁄₂₄ oz. (4 dashes)	1.25 ml
¹⁄₁₂ oz. (approx. half barspoon)	2.5 ml
⅛ oz.	3.75 ml
⅙ oz. (approx. one barspoon)	5 ml
¼ oz.	7.5 ml
⅓ oz.	10 ml
⅖ oz.	12.5 ml
½ oz.	15 ml
⅔ oz.	20 ml
¾ oz.	22.5 ml
⅚ oz.	25 ml
1 oz.	30 ml
1 ⅙ oz.	35 ml
1 ¼ oz.	37.5 ml
1 ⅓ oz.	40 ml
1 ½ oz.	45 ml

1 ⅔ oz.	50 ml
1 ¾ oz.	52.5 ml
1 ⅘ oz.	55 ml
2 oz.	60 ml
2 ⅙ oz.	65 ml
2 ¼ oz.	67.5 ml
2 ⅓ oz.	70 ml
2 ½ oz.	75 ml
2 ⅔ oz.	80 ml
2 ⅘ oz.	85 ml
3 oz.	90 ml
3 ⅓ oz.	100 ml
3 ½ oz.	105 ml
3 ⅔ oz.	110 ml
4 oz.	120 ml

THE COCKTAILS

BODY HORROR
Japanese Slipper

Horror, at its most potent, gives form and dimension to our deepest fears. The creature in the dark. The haunted house. The unstoppable figure with a knife. This is why corruption of the body is such a common theme: we fear decay, disease, and any form of uncontrollable transformation, perhaps because we know that one day, one of these threats might actually become real to us.

Such corporeal anxieties were at their height in 1986 amid the emerging and devastating health crisis triggered by HIV and AIDS; and of all the films made during that era, those collective anxieties were most vividly reflected by the remake of the creaky Vincent Price B movie *The Fly*.

David Cronenberg's version followed scientist Seth Brundle (Jeff Goldblum, pre-irony) as a Dr. Frankenstein who makes a monster out of himself, transforming into the grotesque "Brundlefly." The film is repulsive not because of its special effects but because it changes the original story from an instantaneous transformation to a slow, putrescent metamorphosis. This excruciating change is similarly what makes it a moving, tragic love story.

It's serendipity that the Japanese Slipper also made its first appearance in the mid-80s. In other circumstances, this elegant cocktail might have looked more like a healthy smoothie, but imbibed while watching *The Fly*, however, its oozy muskmelon green is positively disgusting.

THE FLY 1986 DIRECTED BY DAVID CRONENBERG STARRING JEFF GOLDBLUM, GEENA DAVIS, JOHN GETZ

1 oz. Midori

1 oz. Cointreau

1 oz. lemon juice

maraschino cherry, to garnish

1 Add all liquid ingredients to a cocktail shaker.

2 Shake until frost forms on the outside of the shaker.

3 Strain into a martini glass.

4 Decorate with the cherry.

BLOODY MARION
Bloody Mary

The shower, the strings, the scream: Marion Crane's death in *Psycho* is such an indelible part of cinema history that it's difficult to appreciate how audacious it was in 1960. Its reputation, in part, is due to the queasy, innovative filmmaking, which includes 78 shots in 45 seconds and is still startling, tricking the viewer into seeing a violent murder which is never actually depicted. What's truly daring though is that Hitchcock kills off his main character—the movie star on the poster—just 47 minutes into the film. For an audience lacking six decades of familiarity with the story, this gear-shift was as shocking as the abbreviated shower.

Alfred Hitchcock's body of work must be viewed within the context of his sadism and treatment of women both on- and off-screen; yet Marion's death hits so hard because of the time we've spent getting to know her. We empathize with her doomed affair and her bad decision. As she steps into the shower, the guilt has gone; she's decided to return the $40,000 she's stolen from her workplace. She's finally at peace. And then Norman Bates comes along with his "Mommy issues" and decides to take it all away.

With its tomatoes, celery, Worcestershire sauce, and salt and pepper, a Bloody Mary is a third of the way towards a Bolognese, but taste is subjective; and Marion was called Mary in Robert Bloch's original novel, so here we are.

PSYCHO 1960 DIRECTED BY ALFRED HITCHCOCK STARRING ANTHONY PERKINS, JANET LEIGH, VERA MILES

1 ½ oz. vodka

3 oz. tomato juice

½ oz. lemon juice

2 dashes of Worcestershire sauce

2 dashes of Tabasco

grind of pepper

pinch of salt

celery stick, to garnish

1 Add the liquid ingredients and the salt and pepper to a highball glass nearly filled with ice.

2 Stir gently.

3 Garnish with a celery stick.

REDRUM
Planter's Punch

Your brain understands that something isn't right, but not what. In *The Shining*'s early scenes, director Stanley Kubrick clearly defines the Overlook Hotel's layout, and then introduces architectural elements that are impossible: a tree where there can't be a tree, a floor that shouldn't exist, doors that don't lead anywhere. Kubrick's legendary attention to detail insinuates that perhaps these spatial impossibilities are somehow intentional. The effect is disorienting and gives the subconscious impression that the hotel is disturbed in some crucial way. The many ghosts are just a symptom—it's in the walls, in its very foundations. The elevators *bleed*.

Built sacrilegiously on a Native American burial site (in the film, not Stephen King's original novel), the Overlook is a hotel with a bad history, and at the heart of it all is Room 237; psychically agitated and throbbing with sinister energy. Midway through the film, Jack Torrance (Jack Nicholson) enters the room to find a naked woman waiting for him. As they kiss, she transforms into an old lady covered with sores, simultaneously dead in a bathtub and lurching towards him. Although her presence is explained in the novel, the moment's power derives from its ambiguity. This is why the film has attracted obsessive, conspiratorial analysis since its release: it's a mystery with no solution. *The Shining* absorbs meaning because it's incomplete.

THE SHINING 1980 DIRECTED BY STANLEY KUBRICK STARRING JACK NICHOLSON, SHELLEY DUVALL, DANNY LLOYD

½ oz. dark rum	1 Add all the liquid ingredients to a cocktail shaker.
½ oz. light rum	
⅓ oz. orange Curaçao	2 Shake well.
1 oz. orange juice	3 Strain into a hurricane glass filled with ice.
1 oz. pineapple juice	4 Garnish with the mixed fruit.
⅓ oz. lime juice	
⅓ oz. grenadine	
⅓ oz. simple syrup	
a dash of Angostura bitters	
mixed fruits (e.g., an orange slice, pineapple wedge, and a cherry), to garnish	

AN ACTUAL ZOMBIE
Zombie

DAWN OF THE DEAD 1978 DIRECTED BY GEORGE A. ROMERO STARRING DAVID EMGE, KEN FOREE, GAYLEN ROSS

It's already too late. While the men on the television argue about why the dead have come back to life, the truth is it no longer matters. *Dawn of the Dead* begins just as the world slips past the point of no return, with nothing left to do except survive—for as long as you can.

A decade after *Night of the Living Dead*, one of the seminal works of modern horror filmmaker, George A. Romero returned to his zombie apocalypse theme for a sequel which expanded its scope and bleak satirical ambition. As both the living and the dead gravitate inexorably towards a shopping mall, Romero suggests that rampant consumerism is the only part of the zombies that outlives death: "They're after the place. They don't know why, they just remember. Remember that they want to be in here."

While this cocktail provides limited social commentary and it's unlikely that Italian filmmaker Dario Argento will want to substantially reedit it for an international foreign-language release, it does have the benefit of being an actual Zombie: A pre-war Tiki cocktail that gives a romanticized impression of Polynesian culture. Zombies (the drinks) are additionally and thrillingly also known as "skull-punchers." This also happens to be sound advice for confronting Zombies (the undead).

1 ½ oz. Jamaican dark rum	1 Fill a blender with ice.
1 ½ oz. gold rum	2 Add all liquid ingredients.
1 oz. Demerara rum	3 Pulse for a few seconds.
0.7 oz. lime juice	4 Serve in a highball glass.
½ oz. falernum	5 Garnish with mint leaves.
0.3 oz. yellow grapefruit juice	
0.15 oz. cinnamon syrup	
1 tsp. grenadine syrup	
a dash Angostura bitters	
6 drops Pernod	
a few mint leaves, to garnish	

RASPBERRY RIPLEY
Raspberry Martini

ALIEN 1979 DIRECTED BY RIDLEY SCOTT STARRING SIGOURNEY WEAVER, TOM SKERRITT, JOHN HURT

Arriving only a decade after the first Moon landing, *Alien* radically depicted space travel as a working-class profession; an evolution of industrial haulage populated with grumbling, underpaid employees, rather than intrepid test pilots. It's notable that when we first meet the crew of the *Nostromo*, blearily stirring from their hyper-sleep, they're in their underwear: by making its characters ordinary, it leaves them unprotected.

Out of a cast of character actors emerged one of the great heroes of her era: Ellen Ripley (Sigourney Weaver). Audiences cared for her not because of her iconic enemies, but due to her intelligence, cunning and compassion: even with a limited understanding of the impending threat, Ripley is wise enough to decide that the *Nostromo* should follow quarantine protocols and not let John Hurt's compromised Kane back on the ship.

For her climatic battle against the Xenomorph, Ripley is again undressed. In any other horror movie where a "final girl" faces the killer eliminating her companions, this would seem exploitative, but the impression here is of her significant vulnerability. In the corresponding fight in the film's expansive sequel *Aliens*, Ripley would have an exoskeleton and badass, righteous determination; here, she just has her wits and her tenacity.

If Ripley was to ever get some blessed downtime, or at least an evening without being hunted by an endoparasitic creature with acid blood and a bad attitude, then perhaps she'd enjoy this drink named in her honor.

Ingredients	Instructions
½ oz. simple syrup	1. Add the simple syrup and 10 raspberries to a cocktail shaker and muddle the raspberries until they're pulpy.
12 raspberries	
½ oz. Chambord	2. Fill the shaker with ice.
4 oz. vodka	3. Add the Chambord and vodka and shake.
	4. Strain into a martini glass.
	5. Add a couple of raspberries to the rim or skewer them on a toothpick and serve on top.

MOTHER'S RUIN
Bee's Knees

ROSEMARY'S BABY 1968 DIRECTED BY ROMAN POLANSKI STARRING MIA FARROW, JOHN CASSAVETES, RUTH GORDON

Her husband tells her she's imagining things. Her doctor says not to read any more books. "Don't listen to your friends, either." Rosemary Woodhouse (Mia Farrow) is impregnated by Satan and imprisoned by a coven, yet the horrors she suffers aren't supernatural but human.

Rosemary's Baby demonstrates a clarity about the psychological manipulation of women that makes it as relevant now as it was in 1968 (and it is significantly complicated, of course, by the still-unresolved legal charges against its director Roman Polanski).

Rosemary's unequivocal conviction that something's wrong with her own body is undermined by those around her, and she's coerced into rejecting her instinct until it's too late. The only people who don't view her as a vessel are systematically cut out of her life, leaving her increasingly isolated. Her own desires are dismissed, and when she complains, she's accused of being difficult. And the worst part, the ghoulish punch line, is that her actor husband Guy (John Cassavetes) values Rosemary's personhood so little that his prize for selling her to the devil is a part in a Broadway play. And it's not even the lead!

2 tsp. honey
2 tsp. warm water
¾ oz. lemon juice
¾ oz. orange juice
1 ¾ oz. dry gin
twist of lemon, to garnish

1 In a bowl, stir the honey and water until blended.

2 Add the honey syrup, lemon juice, and orange juice into a cocktail shaker; fill the shaker with ice.

3 Add the gin.

4 Shake well.

5 Strain into a chilled coupe cocktail glass.

6 Garnish with a lemon twist.

A NICE CHIANTI
Cardinal

While *The Silence of the Lambs* stolidly follows the young, tenacious FBI agent-in-training Clarice Starling (Jodie Foster) on her first case, Hannibal Lecter looms over the story to such an extent that Anthony Hopkins won the Academy Award for Best Actor for his performance, and the character was named by the American Film Institute as the greatest villain in American cinema. He is in the film for just 16 minutes.

This is a testament, of course, to a memorable performance in an exceptional film, but it also demonstrates the unique hold that Hannibal Lecter has on the public imagination. More than Dracula even, Lecter is horror's great seducer, rearranging the atoms in your body so that you eventually share his worldview. We come to envy him because although he's a monster, he is perfectly at ease with himself; so confident in his aesthetic sensibility that he's delighted to kill for it. Even when you arrest him and lock him in a cell, he seems to be exactly where he intends to be.

Lecter's moral transgression is thrilling to watch because his targets are such brilliant but vulnerable paragons-of-virtue: both Clarice Starling and Will Graham are fascinated by him and not quite as repulsed as they should be. This dynamic turned the fantastically baroque series *Hannibal* into one of the great erotic stories of its period despite—or because of—its obliqueness and reserve.

The fear Hannibal Lecter arouses isn't that he might cook your bodily organs and eat them (although he absolutely will if you're rude), but that he might remove an even deeper part of yourself, and you will like it.

½ oz. crème de cassis

2 ½ oz. Chianti or other red wine

1 Pour the crème de cassis into a martini glass.

2 Top off with the Chianti.

THE SILENCE OF THE LAMBS 1991 DIRECTED BY JONATHAN DEMME STARRING JODIE FOSTER, ANTHONY HOPKINS, SCOTT GLENN

THE TEXAS COCKTAIL MASSACRE
Texas Tea

THE TEXAS CHAINSAW MASSACRE 1974 DIRECTED BY TOBE HOOPER STARRING MARILYN BURNS, EDWIN NEAL, GUNNAR HANSEN

"Who will survive and what will be left of them?" asks the poster of *The Texas Chainsaw Massacre*. It's one of the most enticing and sensational questions in cinema's history. You're afraid to find out the answer, but you know you have to.

Many horror films have tried to give themselves a little juice by claiming to be a true story, but *The Texas Chainsaw Massacre* actively feels dangerous. You trust your own eyes: it's clear that the weather really is punishing, the actors are miserable and dirty, and the ones playing the killers are actually going a little mad. The cinematography is loose, the lighting minimal. There's nothing that looks like a set. Sally (Marilyn Burns) has clearly ended up in a real dilapidated house. A studio movie *couldn't* look like this. You can almost smell the rotting animal carcasses.

The Texas Chainsaw Massacre has an immediacy that's a kind of sick miracle. It feels like you're the one who took a wrong turn and ended up in a bad part of the country, and yet the film is less explicit than the memory of it. In the infamous scene where Leatherface (Gunnar Hansen) impales a victim on a meat hook, you never actually see anything happen, and yet you assume you have. The graphic part of the film isn't the violence, but the terror caused by the violence. In the end, Sally does survive; screaming maniacally as Leatherface wheels his chainsaw around and a pickup truck rockets her away. But what's left of her?

½ oz. tequila	1 Add all the ingredients except the cola into a highball glass filled with ice.
½ oz. rum	
½ oz. vodka	2 Stir well.
½ oz. gin	3 Top with the cola.
½ oz. bourbon	4 Stir again.
½ oz. triple sec	
½ oz. lemon juice	
½ oz. simple syrup	
4 oz. cola	

CORPSE REVIVER
Corpse Reviver No.2

FRANKENSTEIN 1931 DIRECTED BY JAMES WHALE STARRING BORIS KARLOFF, COLIN CLIVE, VALERIE HOBSON

Mary Shelley's creation of *Frankenstein* is nearly as famous as the creation of the monster itself. During 1816, the "Year Without a Summer" thanks to a volcanic eruption, Mary (then Godwin) and Percy Shelley were vacationing in Switzerland when their host Lord Byron suggested a diverting indoor activity: everyone would write a ghost story. The fruits of Mary's efforts became one of the seminal works of horror literature, and possibly the first ever science-fiction novel. She was only 18 years old.

Two centuries later the book retains its eerie power, despite the fact that Victor Frankenstein has a frustrating tendency to faint for months anytime the action gets going. Frankenstein is the prototypical mad scientist, but the disquieting thing is that he *isn't* mad. Instead, his rationality makes him the embodiment of man's hubris: he spends two years obsessed with retrieving life from death without ever thinking of the ramifications. Moments after finally achieving his goal and beholding his creation's watery eyes and straight black lips, he concludes, "the beauty of the dream vanished, and breathless horror and disgust filled my heart," and runs off.

Everyone he cares about eventually pays the price.

James Whale's 1931 adaptation has commandeered the popular recollection of the tale—Frankenstein doesn't even have an assistant in the novel, let alone a hunchback—but its narrative tidiness is less satisfying. Shelley doesn't give her creature the easy excuse of a criminal's brain but suggests that perhaps the very act of giving him life was a sin.

Shelley is astute to never specify what "instruments of life" Frankenstein employs in his efforts but given that the corpse reviver cocktail emerged a few decades after the book's publication, it's not inconceivable that he was using gin and Cointreau.

Ingredients
1 oz. gin
1 oz. Cointreau
1 oz. Lillet Blonde
1 oz. lemon juice
dash of absinthe
twist of orange, to garnish

1 Add the liquid ingredients into a cocktail shaker filled with ice.

2 Shake well.

3 Strain into a chilled coupe glass.

4 Garnish with an orange twist.

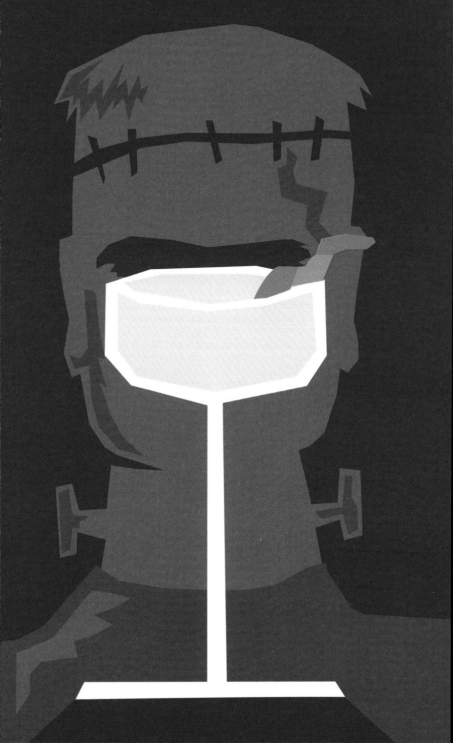

THE POWER OF MIAMI ICED TEA COMPELS YOU!

Miami Iced Tea

THE EXORCIST 1973 DIRECTED BY WILLIAM FRIEDKIN STARRING ELLEN BURSTYN, MAX VON SYDOW, LINDA BLAIR

Right around 1967, a small window opened in time. Struggling to engage with a disillusioned counterculture, movie studios gave unprecedented freedom to young filmmakers, who grasped the opportunity to make numerous classics: ambitious, stylistically daring films for adults. Blockbusters would follow, and authorial vision would falter under its own ostentation, but for a time, American cinema was abloom.

In horror, a parallel movement took place: an oasis between the end of the restrictive Production Code and the rise of special effects, relying on mood and suspense with isolated eruptions of terror. Of this brood, *The Exorcist* was the true phenomenon, becoming the first horror film nominated for the Oscar for Best Picture. It gained a reputation as a film *so* scary that people fainted and vomited from the shock. Ambulances parked outside some cinemas to deal with the fallout.

A modern viewer might be surprised to find that for much of its running time *The Exorcist* is a family drama, but that also played into its power, slowly building toward its famous exorcism scene with possessed teenager Regan (Linda Blair). While extreme responses like heart attacks weren't necessarily the film's responsibility, mass hysteria is real: if an audience believes they're going to watch something so extreme that it'll affect them physically, and if they've spent hours eagerly queuing for the experience, then when the lights finally go down, something can actually happen.

½ oz. vodka	1 Add the vodka, gin, rum, triple sec, peach schnapps, and cranberry juice into a cocktail shaker filled with ice.
½ oz. gin	
½ oz. light rum	
½ triple sec	2 Shake lightly.
½ oz. peach schnapps	3 Strain into a highball glass.
1 oz. cranberry juice	4 Top with the lemon-lime soda.
lemon-lime soda	5 Garnish with a lime wedge.
wedge of lime, to garnish	

AN AMERICAN COCKTAIL IN LONDON
Sazerac

AN AMERICAN WEREWOLF IN LONDON 1981 DIRECTED BY JOHN LANDIS STARRING DAVID NAUGHTON, JENNY AGUTTER, GRIFFIN DUNNE

Horror can be so baroque and outlandish that it only takes a nudge to become funny. Humor is integral to some of the genre's most effective films, intensifying a strained moment or deflating tension. *An American Werewolf in London* is a comedy even at its goriest, but that then makes its one serious moment genuinely disconcerting.

As David (David Naughton) recuperates from a werewolf attack that killed his best friend, the scene moves to his family living room. At first, you assume it's a flashback. David works at the table while his mother washes dishes. His siblings sprawl out in front of the TV. A simple idyll. But then there's a knock at the door. Mutant Nazis burst in. They hold a knife to David's throat and make him watch as they fire machine-gun rounds into his family. They set the house ablaze and then kill him too. They seem *giddy*.

What to make of this? The sequence is a true nightmare—the idea that at any point the world might turn on you. Writer-director John Landis was born only five years after the end of World War II. It's not an abstract fear. This scene—in the middle of an irreverent horror-comedy—reveals it as an inadvertently significant reflection on the postwar experience of Jewish Americans.

½ oz. absinthe (or Herbsaint)	1 Swirl absinthe around a chilled old-fashioned glass and fill with crushed ice.
2 ½ oz. cognac	
2 dashes Peychaud's Bitters	2 Add the cognac, bitters, and sugar cube to a mixing glass filled with ice.
1 sugar cube	
slice of lemon	3 Stir the contents of the mixing glass gently, dissolving the sugar cube.
	4 Discard the excess absinthe and ice from the old-fashioned glass.
	5 Strain the drink into the glass.
	6 Wipe the rim with the lemon slice.

WE ALL ROOT BEER FLOAT DOWN HERE
Root beer float

IT CHAPTER ONE 2017 DIRECTED BY ANDY MUSCHIETTI STARRING BILL SKARSGÅRD, JAEDEN LIEBERHER, SOPHIA LILLIS

The bulk of Stephen King's novels and stories exist within the same literary multiverse: over a dozen take place in the fictional Maine town Castle Rock alone, while his *Dark Tower* series spent 30 years tying together everything from *Salem's Lot* to a fictionalized version of King himself. In the mouth of all these parallel universes, Derry is the rotten tooth: home to an ancient cosmic evil that lives in the sewers and appears periodically to devour children.

Mapping the layers of connection between the town and King's sprawling canon requires complicated diagrams, but the peculiar thing is that *It*, his primary book about Derry, similarly lies within a confluence of influences. The original 1986 novel was the apogee of many of King's narrative tics as well as a tribute to his formative passions from classic horror movies to Lovecraftian cosmic horror.

Years later, the television series *Stranger Things*, while also ransacking everything from *Freaks and Geeks* to *Under the Skin*, primarily riffed on the author's work (King himself described it as "Steve King's Greatest Hits") and *It* most of all. But then, in the flush of *Stranger Things*' global popularity, studios and networks rushed to develop King adaptations, including a two-part version of *It* which went as far as using that series' Finn Wolfhard in a main role as part of the original group of friends that his *Stranger Things* group of friends was inspired by. In the end, *It* became a copy of a copy of itself, which is exactly the sort of mind-bending nonsense that Stephen King loves.

2 oz. Kahlúa	1	Add the Kahlúa and Irish cream to a chilled beer stein or float glass.
1 oz. Irish cream liqueur		
1 scoop of vanilla ice cream	2	Carefully drop the ice cream into the glass.
root beer	3	Top the glass with root beer, pouring slowly at an angle.
whipped cream, to garnish		
maraschino cherry, to garnish	4	Garnish with whipped cream, a maraschino cherry, and a paper straw.

IT FOLLOWS*
Boilermaker

From its very first second on screen, *It Follows* unsettles. As a young woman desperately scrambles to escape from some unseen threat, the sound track buzzes and thrums in a manner that's disorientating, unbearable, and thrilling in equal measure. Teeming with subtext and possible allegorical readings, *It Follows* marked horror's first signs of life after the dominance of "torture porn" and a glut of tired sequels; what followed *It Follows* was a fruitful decade of thoughtful, lucid horror.

The premise is elegant in its simplicity. After having sex on a date, Jay (Maika Monroe) learns that she has what might be best described as a supernatural STD: a shape-shifting figure in constant pursuit, which will kill her unless she has sex with someone new to pass the infection along. But if they die before this happens, the scourge reverts back to her. What plays out feels like the worst sort of bad dream, as adolescent sexual anxiety is reshaped into unnatural renditions of friends, family, and hideous strangers: a monster that cannot be stopped, only evaded, and one which will eventually catch up with you, sooner or later.

Speaking of chasers: a boilermaker is one of the simplest cocktails to make, and benefits from being easy to vary. It can be revelatory to combine a whiskey and beer with complementary flavors, but you can also just use whatever you have around. However, if you're being pursued by a mutating sex entity, you probably shouldn't dawdle.

1 ½ oz. whiskey	1 Fill a shot glass with whiskey.
12 oz. beer	2 Fill a pint glass with beer.
	3 Drink the whiskey.
	4 Drink the beer.

Alternately, you can drop the shot glass straight into the beer, or if you're feeling bold, maneuver the filled shot glass into the empty pint glass before filling it with beer. Live your life.

*Except "It" is a beer chaser, and not the violent psychic manifestation of sexual shame

MIDNIGHT SUN
Snowball

THE THING 1982 DIRECTED BY JOHN CARPENTER STARRING KURT RUSSELL, WILFORD BRIMLEY, KEITH DAVID

John Carpenter's remake of *The Thing from Another World* works so well because it understands the uncomfortable vagueness of the word "thing." A named antagonist has properties and capabilities that can be understood, if not easily overcome. The shape-shifting creature in *The Thing*, on the other hand, can be anything, or anyone. The terror it inspires comes not from any specific form but its unknowability.

How do you fight something you can't even define?

Uncertainty becomes deep paranoia as the crew of U.S. *Outpost #31* come to this terrible realization, and fear then infiltrates the group as successfully as the Thing itself.

The life-form's most gruesome outing occurs as the research station's physician applies a defibrillator to one of his colleagues. The patient's chest subsequently changes into a mouth and bites the doctor's arms off, before going through a hideous transformation into a spider-like severed head.

After such bizarre and disquieting events, the only rational response is the film's most famous line: "You've got to be fucking kidding."

In trying times, like being unable to distinguish human from interloper, or just when playing a particularly tough round of computer chess, helicopter pilot MacReady (Kurt Russell) reaches for a bottle of J&B scotch.

A Snowball might have been more appropriate—for the weather, if not the season (it's pretty festive).

0.7 oz. lime juice	1 Fill a collins glass with ice.
3 ½ oz. carbonated lemonade	2 Add the lime juice and lemonade, followed by the Advocaat.
2 oz. Advocaat	3 Lightly stir to mix the ingredients without losing the lemonade's carbonation.

47

DRACULA'S KISS
Vampiro

As the son of a countess and a lieutenant colonel, Christopher Lee was always at his most effective playing characters from aristocratic or privileged backgrounds, whose corruption and malign intent are obscured by their status. In *Lord of the Rings*, Saruman's descent into evil is unthinkable to his fellow wizards; while as Lord Summerisle, the "hiding-in-plain-sight" antagonist of *The Wicker Man*, he is deceptively jovial in a yellow turtleneck and tweeds. His Lordship's refined upbringing convinces you that he must have your best interests at heart, but—in fiction as in real life—this is rarely the case.

Lee remains the definitive Count Dracula because he plays him both as an erotic figure and a slightly melancholy one. Recognizable for his operatic bass voice, imposing stature and menacing, sunken features, the secret of his appeal was his ability to charm audiences as he simultaneously scared them, making darkness and the occult seem oddly seductive, even if it was also deadly. The poster for the first of his seven Dracula pictures for Hammer Films describes him as "the terrifying lover who died—yet lived!" as he leans over a racy victim, his mouth approaching her neck. She seems rapturous at the prospect.

Over his centuries of unliving, Count Dracula narrowed his taste in beverages to just one. If he'd made it as far as South America, however, perhaps he would have discovered the Bloody Maria-adjacent Vampiro. Much-loved in Mexico, it's often sold there at stalls in plastic bags, its bright red liquid sloshing around diabolically.

DRACULA 1958 DIRECTED BY TERENCE FISHER STARRING PETER CUSHING, CHRISTOPHER LEE, MICHAEL GOUGH

2 oz. tequila	1 Add all ingredients except the lime wedge into a cocktail shaker filled with ice.
1 oz. tomato juice	
1 oz. orange juice	2 Shake well.
½ oz. lime juice	3 Strain into a highball glass filled with ice (or use a plastic bag).
½ oz. grenadine	
7 drops of Tabasco	4 Garnish with the lime wedge.
pinch of salt	
grind of black pepper	
lime wedge, to garnish	

SCRÈAM DE MENTHE
Stinger

SCREAM 1996 DIRECTED BY WES CRAVEN STARRING NEVE CAMPBELL, COURTENEY COX, DAVID ARQUETTE

The world was ready for *Scream*. Slasher films became so popular during the 1980s that they'd crowded out most other horror, but the formula was exhausted by endless sequels. In a genre that thrives on the element of surprise, it's difficult to scare an audience when they can anticipate everything that will happen. The time—specifically, the verbose, irony-embracing 1990s—was ripe for a slasher movie that puckishly explored its own conventions.

Scream takes place in a world where all the other horror films exist, and, pivotally, its characters have seen them all. This allowed writer Kevin Williamson to state the genre's rules and then play with them, ensuring a spark of energy whether he subverted them or followed through with them precisely.

At the time, this self-conscious, self-referential attitude was invigorating, and never more so than during its 12-minute opening scene—a deadly phone call which lasts just long enough to convince you that the film's biggest star, Drew Barrymore, is also the protagonist. It retained some of this power for the sequel, rushed out the following year, but by *Scream 3* it was already dated, as much of a formula as the very films it had been exposing.

The series' most successful tweak turned out to be reframing the slasher movie as a whodunnit: the killer, no matter their identity or preposterous reasons for turning to mass slaughter, wasn't a supernatural brute but an acquaintance hiding behind a cheap Halloween mask. This made them more human, and therefore more horrifying.

2 ½ oz. Cognac

1 oz. white crème de menthe

1 mint leaf, to garnish

1. Add the Cognac and crème de menthe to a cocktail shaker.
2. Shake vigorously.
3. Strain into a chilled martini glass (although this drink can also be served over ice in an old-fashioned glass).
4. Garnish with the mint leaf.

HEREDITCHERRY SOUR
Cherry Sour

HEREDITARY 2018 DIRECTED BY ARI ASTER STARRING TONI COLLETTE, MILLY SHAPIRO, GABRIEL BYRNE

The term "Elevated Horror" emerged after the 2015 release of *The Witch*, and was applied to a range of meticulous, thematically rich films from *Hereditary* to *The Babadook* to *Get Out*.

Even though Elevated Horror seems to be mostly brought up in order to denounce it, the idea that there's something different about modern horror has persisted regardless; perhaps as a begrudging acknowledgment that many of today's most talented filmmakers now create horror movies.

Genre fiction has been historically marginalized by critics wary of popular work, but it's always been strange that horror—the most self-reflexive, purely cinematic genre, and the one using every tool of the medium to construct mood and terror—has struggled to get due credit.

The truth is that many of cinema's great filmmakers, from F.W. Murnau to Alfred Hitchcock, have toiled in the genre, while the work of acclaimed art house filmmakers like David Lynch, Lucile Hadžihalilović, and Michael Haneke has often been horror adjacent. The careful tension and social commentary praised in Elevated Horror has been woven into the fabric of the genre since its conception, and even when a horror film has no ambitions beyond scaring an audience, the fears it invokes still speak to its era's apprehensions. The desire to elevate horror suggests, condescendingly and incorrectly, that horror was lower than other genres and needed elevating in the first place.

2 oz. brandy	1 Add the brandy, lemon juice, and simple syrup into a cocktail shaker filled with ice.
¾ oz. lemon juice	
1 oz. simple syrup	2 Shake well.
3 maraschino cherries, to garnish	3 Strain into a delmonico glass.
	4 Garnish with the cherries.

GIALLO SHOTS
Jello Shots

"It's useless to try to explain it to you. You wouldn't understand," Pat Hingle (Eva Axén) says to her friend Sonia (Susanna Javicoli) in the opening sequence of *Suspiria*, "It all seems so absurd, so fantastic." This also happens to be an accurate description of the film the audience is about to watch. Within minutes, Pat has been suffocated against a window, stabbed repeatedly (we somehow see the knife enter her beating heart), dropped through a stained-glass window and hung by a cord, while her friend is both impaled by a spike and has her face split open by a shard of glass. The film is a stranger to subtlety.

Prizing mood over coherence, *Suspiria* is sensational in the pure sense of the word: every inch of the screen is bathed in lurid colors, and its aggressive score (by director Dario Argento with the prog band Goblin) barely rests. In the delirious opening scene, a low voice hisses "Witch! Witch!" as American ballet student Suzy Bannion (Jessica Harper) is still in the taxi on the way to the dance academy/secret coven. As was then customary in Italian cinema, both the English and Italian versions are entirely dubbed, which makes the performances flat and clumsy but fascinatingly unreal.

Despite its supernatural elements, *Suspiria* fits neatly into Italy's tradition of giallo—horror-thrillers which delight in the histrionic murder of beautiful women. It's vulgar, distasteful, ridiculous nonsense—at one point a character doesn't notice that they're jumping straight into a massive pit of razor wires—but also improbably sumptuous and entrancing.

The traditional place and time for a jello shot is during a mistake in your youth, but they can also be made at home. Like the films of Dario Argento, one is probably enough.

SUSPIRIA 1977 DIRECTED BY DARIO ARGENTO STARRING JESSICA HARPER, STEFANIA CASINI, FLAVIO BUCCI

3 oz. gelatin, in your choice of flavor	1 Add the gelatin to 8 oz. of boiling water.
8 oz. boiling water	2 Once dissolved, add the vodka and cold water.
4 oz. vodka, chilled	3 Stir to combine.
4 oz. cold water	4 Pour into approximately 10 plastic shot cups.
	5 Refrigerate for at least 2 hours.
	6 Place the jello shots in a bandolier and sell them at the world's worst nightclub.

MASQUE OF THE RED WINE
Zurracapote

Edgar Allan Poe charted the darkness of man's heart, and thus his endings were brutal. In *The Masque of the Red Death*, Prince Prospero invites a thousand nobles to take sanctuary from a plague in his abbey, welding the doors shut behind them. They decide to have a magnificent ball, which goes well until the arrival of a gaunt, uninvited partygoer. The guests die, one by one, until "Darkness and Decay and the Red Death held illimitable dominion over all." This takes some beating, although let's not forget that Poe also invented the *entire* genre of detective fiction with a story where the killer turned out to be an escaped orangutan.

Similar to Sangria except with a focus on dried fruits over citrus, the Spanish punch Zurracapote is traditionally served during local festivals, so it's ideal if you'd also like to hold a fate-tempting Masquerade ball in your castellated abbey.

Serves 5

4 oz. dried plums

4 oz. raisins

10 oz. peaches

75cl bottle of red wine
(ideally a young, fruity Rioja)

8 oz. brown sugar

peel of one lemon

1 cinnamon stick

1 In a large bowl, cover the plums, raisins, and peaches with warm water and leave to soak for at least 2 hours.

2 Add the wine, brown sugar, lemon peel, and cinnamon to a medium saucepan and bring to a boil. Reduce heat and simmer for 5 minutes, stirring continuously.

3 Drain the liquid from the fruits and discard.

4 Add the fruits to the pan. Cover and simmer gently for 15 minutes. Remove from the heat.

5 Leave the fruits to macerate in the spiced wine ideally for 2 or 3 days, but a couple of hours will suffice if time is short.

6 Remove the cinnamon and lemon peel, leaving the other fruits.

7 Serve warm or cold.

CARRIE'S PROM PUNCH
Bombay Punch

CARRIE 1976 DIRECTED BY BRIAN DE PALMA STARRING SISSY SPACEK, PIPER LAURIE, AMY IRVING

Nearly all of *Carrie*'s best-known scenes—from Carrie's traumatic first period to her prom-night humiliation at the hands of her teenage crush—involve unexpected blood. By necessity, director Brian De Palma moved away from the epistolary structure of Stephen King's novel but retained its emphasis on high school as a conformist hell and puberty as an uncontrollable source of both power and dread.

Peppered with shocks by De Palma, who self-consciously styled himself as the next Alfred Hitchcock (although the true heir turned out to be his friend Steven Spielberg), *Carrie*'s imagery quickly entered pop culture, but its power lies in a hugely vulnerable performance by Sissy Spacek and an enjoyably demented one by Piper Laurie as her zealot mother.

Although Carrie ultimately turns to telekinetic pyromania, the audience still roots for her because she's been backed into a corner, punished for being different, and punished for trying to be the same. When, in the film's often-imitated final scene, her bloody arm reaches out from the rubble of her home, we jump, but we also cheer.

Famously, neither Carrie nor her fellow attendees got to enjoy their prom through to its intended conclusion, but perhaps if they'd had some of this punch then the evening would have gone in a better direction. Try it yourself, first making sure that a young John Travolta isn't lurking around your home with a loose bucket of blood.

Serves 10

8 oz. sweet sherry

8 oz. brandy

1 ½ oz. triple sec

1 ½ oz. maraschino liqueur

a 75 cl bottle of Champagne (Prosecco also works!)

18 oz. club soda

3 oz. simple syrup

slices of orange and lemon, to garnish

1 Add all liquid ingredients to a punch bowl filled with ice.

2 Stir gently.

3 Garnish with orange and lemon slices.

"A BEAUTIFUL NECK"
Horse's Neck

NOSFERATU 1922 DIRECTED BY F.W. MURNAU STARRING MAX SCHRECK, AGRETA SCHRÖDER, GUSTAV VON WANGENHEIM

Some stories become so ingrained within our culture that we think of them as being ageless, but when F. W. Murnau directed *Nosferatu* in 1921, Bram Stoker's *Dracula* had only been published 24 years earlier. It would be like someone making a film today based on some Y2K-phobic techno thriller, or a late '90s YA series about heathen wizard children. Although *Dracula* was first adapted six months before Murnau started filming (in the presumed lost *Drakula Halála)* the story and its characters were still fresh and open for reinterpretation—the now ingrained notion that a vampire must sleep through the day comes from *Nosferatu* rather than the novel.

Character names were changed for the adaptation, possibly for copyright reasons, or perhaps just because it was for a German audience, but this has since allowed Count Orlok (Max Schreck) to become a distinct character in his own right even though he's essentially a supermarket-own-brand Dracula. Orlok's design has a weird verisimilitude that makes him look like those old photographs that purport to show ghosts: *Shadow of the Vampire*, 2000's fictionalized account of *Nosferatu*'s production, imagines a scenario where Schreck was an actual vampire persuaded to star in *Nosferatu* with this information kept from the imperiled cast and crew. The idea isn't totally preposterous. If the film had been shot later with different cameras, Orlok would look goofy, but in fragile, early black-and-white, he's eerily convincing.

1 ⅓ oz. Cognac	
4 oz. ginger ale	
dash of Angostura bitters	
long spiral of lemon peel, to garnish	

1 Pour the Cognac and ginger ale into a highball glass filled with ice cubes.

2 Stir gently.

3 Add a dash of bitters.

4 Dangle the long spiral of lemon peel into the glass—this can be tricky so you may want to do it at the start.

FROM DUSK TEQUILA DAWN
Tequila Sunrise

FROM DUSK TILL DAWN 1996 DIRECTED BY ROBERT RODRIGUEZ STARRING HARVEY KEITEL, GEORGE CLOONEY, JULIETTE LEWIS

Although it often came at the expense of tension, practical horror effects were at their most vibrant and gleefully revolting during the 1980s. The goal of artists like Rob Bottin and Rick Baker wasn't just to terrify but to entertain: the creatures and gore they designed were always fascinating to behold, disgusting in a manner that was delightful rather than disturbing. They arrived during an era where the genre shifted away from psychological dread and instead, embraced cheap, lurid thrills.

Horror movies, and specifically horror movies of the 1980s, are the only place where a makeup artist could become an icon. Tom Savini, the prosthetic makeup artist who worked with George A. Romero on films including *Dawn of the Dead* and *Creepshow*, became better known than his peers because of his willingness to appear in the films that he was providing gruesome effects for.

Savini soon became known as "The Sultan of Splatter," revered among a certain breed of film fans that included Quentin Tarantino and Robert Rodriguez. By 1996, they'd become the hippest filmmakers in Hollywood, and Rodriguez was directing Tarantino's script *From Dusk Till Dawn*; a garrulous crime thriller that veers off the road to become a vampire B-movie. Newly powerful—the film marks the brief period where Tarantino was a viable co-star to George Clooney—in their first loving tribute to grind house, who else would they cast as a biker called Sex Machine but Tom Savini?

1 ½ oz. tequila	
3 oz. orange juice	
½ oz. grenadine	
orange slice, to garnish	
maraschino cherry, to garnish	

1 Add the tequila and orange juice into a highball glass filled with ice.

2 Carefully pour the grenadine on top. It will sink to create the sunrise effect, don't stir.

3 Garnish with an orange slice and a maraschino cherry.

THE OMINOUS TOUCAN
Jungle Bird

THE BIRDS 1963 DIRECTED BY ALFRED HITCHCOCK STARRING ROD TAYLOR, TIPPI HEDREN, JESSICA TANDY

Alfred Hitchcock was never shy about using cinema to force others into sharing in his personal terrors. Birds aren't especially scary—until you do something they don't like. *The Birds* strays from Daphne du Maurier's original story both narratively and geographically while keeping the central idea: every bird, for no apparent reason, goes into a frenzy and starts killing humans. This idea is ludicrous but underlines something deeply troubling. Birds can't be understood, or reasoned with, and there are 400 billion of them.

Hitchcock casts the everyday in an unpleasant new light, avoiding birds of prey in favor of seagulls and wood pigeons. He takes a perverse delight in the damage birds can do; nicking at children's ears, faces and hands, drawing blood. It's understandable that its once cutting-edge special effects haven't aged well, and 60 years later the scenes of eerie anticipation are more chilling: *The Birds*' definitive image is a murder of crows perched upon every bar of a climbing frame, silent, watching, waiting.

This cocktail is inspired by the Jungle Bird, which originates from the Kuala Lumpur Hilton. Its hotel bar was named The Aviary as the guests could watch birds through the window; fortunately, they didn't go insane and dive-bomb the patrons before this drink could be invented.

1 ½ oz. dark rum	
¾ oz. Campari	
4 oz. pineapple juice	
½ oz. lime juice	
½ oz. simple syrup	
1 maraschino cherry, to garnish	
1 pineapple wedge, to garnish	

1   Add liquid ingredients to a cocktail shaker filled with ice.

2   Shake thoroughly.

3   Strain into an old-fashioned glass filled with crushed ice.

4   Garnish with a cherry and a pineapple wedge, preferably shaped to resemble plumage.*

*Traditionally, you're also supposed to garnish this drink with an orchid, but come on, this is mid-tier Hitchcock, not *Vertigo*.

THE TURN OF THE SCREWDRIVER

Screwdriver

THE TURN OF THE SCREW 1992 DIRECTED BY RUSTY LEMORANDE STARRING PATSY KENSIT, STÉPHANE AUDRAN, JULIAN SANDS

The walls between life and death seemed thinner during the Victorian era. Of the many ghost stories that came from that fulsome period, encouraged by the rise of the periodical press and a fashion for spiritualism, why do we keep revisiting *The Turn of the Screw*? Since its 12-part publication in *Collier's Weekly* in 1898, successive generations have translated Henry James' story into plays, films, assorted television miniseries, a ballet, a chamber opera, and dozens upon dozens of other adaptations, both direct and free-flowing.

A restrained and chilling story about a governess minding two orphaned children, who comes to believe that a country house is haunted by the previous governess and her valet lover, *The Turn of the Screw* is one of literature's most closely interpreted ghost stories. It's often approached as a puzzle to be solved because so much is left tantalizingly unanswered: we never learn why the boy Miles was expelled from school, or what corrupting events may have transpired between the ghosts and the children, although there's the intimation of a relationship abusively continued beyond the grave, using possession.

The Turn of the Screw's prestige rests on its finely calibrated ambiguity: a ghost story where the actual ghosts are only ever seen by the narrator. Is the governess trying to protect her charges from the parasitic intentions of malevolent spirits, or projecting her own sexual repression onto two ghostly shapes? The story has perhaps resounded for so long because it was constructed to make both answers valid and each, in their own fashion, equally haunting.

---

1 ½ oz. vodka

8 oz. orange juice (preferably freshly squeezed)

slice of orange, to garnish

1   Add the vodka to a highball glass, filled with ice.

2   Pour in the orange juice.

3   Stir gently.

4   Garnish with a slice of orange.

A HAMMER AND A NAIL
Rusty Nail

THE DEVIL RIDES OUT 1968 DIRECTED BY TERENCE FISHER STARRING CHRISTOPHER LEE, CHARLES GRAY, NIKE ARRIGHI

Hammer Films made 158 films between 1947 and the year the company entered liquidation in 1979, in every popular genre, but gained its reputation from its championing of Gothic horror. These modestly budgeted productions often shared the same sets, cast, and crew and accordingly shared a sensibility. They reinvigorated classic monsters by being faithful to their source material and boasted stars like Peter Cushing, Christopher Lee, and Ingrid Pitt who understood the sincere, macabre tone perfectly.

To become popular for an aesthetic also means to eventually become outdated for it and it's remarkable to think that *The Devil Rides Out* and *Rosemary's Baby* were made during the same year; they may as well have come from different centuries. Both deal with a hidden satanic cult, but one was adapted from a dusty novel by a reactionary author—there's no sex or violence, Christianity saves the day, and the moral universe remains intact—and the other from the previous year's slick, achingly-modern best seller set in contemporary New York.

The distance between the two foreshadows the demise of Hammer a decade later, yet the quaint, tame charms of *The Devil Rides Out* (renamed *The Devil's Bride* in America, presumably so audiences wouldn't think it was a western) have come back around. There's a simple pleasure in watching Christopher Lee, in a rare heroic role as the Duc de Richleau, walk around lavish mansions knowing everything. It takes De Richleau minutes to deduce that his friend is joining a cult, while it's never remotely explained why he has an encyclopedic knowledge of satanic rituals and can intuit information like, "Obviously, Mocata is one of the great adepts. Perhaps even an Ipsissimus!" off the top of his head.

Lee's clearly having an excellent time, and whenever he's on screen, so do we.

2 oz. whiskey	1 Add the whiskey into an old-fashioned glass, filled with ice.
¾ oz. Drambuie	2 Pour the Drambuie on top.
twist of lemon, to garnish	3 Stir gently.
	4 Garnish with a lemon twist.

THE MAY QUEEN
May Blossom Fizz

MIDSOMMAR 2019 DIRECTED BY ARI ASTER STARRING FLORENCE PUGH, JACK REYNOR, VILHELM BLOMGREN

By the time Ari Aster made his feature debut *Hereditary*, his aesthetic had already been fully formed through a series of chilling short films, so his follow-up, *Midsommar*, was an assured continuation of key themes and techniques rather than the big, messy swing that often defines a sophomore film. Despite the focus shifting to a secretive community in Sweden, Aster maintained his interest in portentous harbingers—the history of the occult, family tragedy, the spontaneous eruption of unusual, nauseating deaths, and, most critically, cults with hidden designs on the protagonist. *Midsommar* was both new and more of the same, but what it did add was an extraordinary sense of catharsis.

In horror, catharsis usually comes from the survival of a threat or the threat's outright defeat. These can both be tremendously powerful but exist within the context of the film's narrative: they're a thing that happens so that the movie can end, and we can all go home. The equivalent moment in *Midsommar* is far stranger and more effective.

After her life collapses due to a violent tragedy, Dani Ardor (Florence Pugh) follows her unsupportive boyfriend Christian (Jack Reynor) and his friends to a remote commune for a once-every-90-years midsummer celebration. A series of distressing, bizarre, and psychedelic events occur, and she has a panic attack after witnessing a betrayal. What happens next is unexpectedly affecting: the commune's young women enclose themselves around her, moving, sobbing, and screaming as one, sharing the burden of her trauma. It's a moment of release that can't be matched by the besting of any mere movie monster.

¾ oz. lemon juice	1 Add the lemon juice, punsch, and grenadine into a cocktail shaker filled with ice.
2 oz. Swedish punsch	
1 oz. grenadine	2 Shake well.
club soda	3 Strain into an old-fashioned glass, filled with ice.
A few edible flowers (optional), to garnish	4 Top with club soda.
	5 Stir.
	6 Decorate with as many flowers as you like.

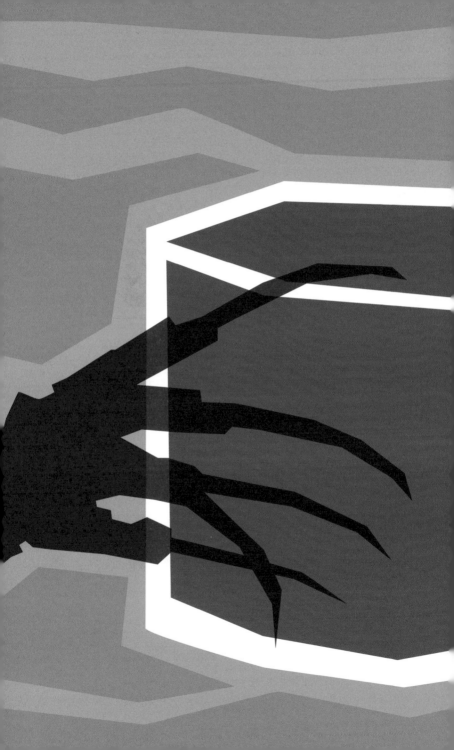

AN ILL-ADVISED NIGHTCAP
Hot Toddy

Freddy Krueger, the bastard son of a hundred maniacs, stood out from his slasher movie contemporaries because he actually seemed to be having a good time. While his fellow murderers Jason Voorhees, Michael Myers, and Leatherface were silent, traumatized man-children, Krueger made bad puns, danced around in his stripey sweater, and toyed with the very fabric of reality.

Freddy didn't stalk his victims with a knife; he'd turn into a television, smash their head into the screen, and welcome them to prime time. Sometimes, he'd dress up as a bus driver, or a French waiter, or a motorcycle, for no apparent reason other than his own amusement. He wasn't scary, but that was never really the point.

After six films in seven years, Krueger had become a live-action cartoon. The only novelty that remained was how outlandish his kills would be. It took Wes Craven, the writer-director of the first *A Nightmare on Elm Street*, to return the series to its compelling original premise: the existential threat isn't a man with bladed gloves, but being no longer able to distinguish between real life and imagination.

The result was one of the most quietly influential films of its era. *Wes Craven's New Nightmare* portended the self-referential horror boom that would arrive with his next outing, *Scream*, and still reverberates through the genre.

1 tbsp. honey

1 oz. whiskey*

¼ lemon

a cup of black tea

*Rum and brandy would also work, although for a brandy hot toddy, substitute a teaspoon of sugar instead of the honey.

1 Pour the honey in a glass.

2 Add the whiskey.

3 Add the juice from the lemon (watch out for seeds).

4 Top with hot tea.

WES CRAVEN'S NEW NIGHTMARE 1994. DIRECTED BY WES CRAVEN. STARRING HEATHER LANGENKAMP, ROBERT ENGLUND, JEFF DAVIS

LET'S GO CAMPING!
Bramble

THE BLAIR WITCH PROJECT 1999   DIRECTED BY DANIEL MYRICK, EDUARDO SÁNCHEZ   STARRING HEATHER DONAHUE, MICHAEL C. WILLIAMS

There's a primordial fizz to the most basic horror stories that makes them compelling even after centuries of retelling. Someone believes their home is haunted. A couple take a wrong turn. Kids get lost in the woods and find they're not alone. Such tales draw from Western European folklore; obsessed with the magical potency of forests and the dangerous things that happen in them. They're very old, which makes them ideal for putting into new frames.

The Blair Witch Project was the earliest triumph of viral film marketing, with initial hype suggesting that the film really did comprise recovered footage and that its subjects were actually missing. By the time it reached cinemas, audiences were well aware that this was just a movie after all, but it was hard to shake the feeling that the actors weren't entirely in on the fact.

This approach wouldn't have worked without unknown performers or non-improvised dialogue. Under extreme stress, Heather Donahue, Mike Williams, and Josh Leonard are often shrill. They don't have witty banter; they're just regular people, succumbing to paranoia. The film's backlash came swiftly due to its evasiveness, but now, divorced from the "scariest movie ever" label, that's what makes it effective. On such a low budget, its effects would have signaled that it was fiction, but instead, the dread carefully seeps in as the trio make wrong choice after wrong choice. *The Blair Witch Project* doesn't show anything more explicit than a man standing against a wall and made a quarter of a billion dollars.

---

2 oz. gin

1 oz. lemon juice

½ oz. simple syrup

¾ oz. crème de mûre

2 blackberries, to garnish

1 Add the gin, lemon juice, and simple syrup into a cocktail shaker filled with ice.

2 Shake well.

3 Strain into a chilled, old-fashioned glass filled with crushed ice.

4 Pour the crème de mûre in a circular motion so that it seeps into the drink.

5 Garnish with the blackberries.

THE WICKER MAN(HATTAN)
Manhattan

THE WICKER MAN 1973 DIRECTED BY ROBIN HARDY STARRING EDWARD WOODWARD, CHRISTOPHER LEE, DIANE CILENTO

A complicated fate entraps some films whereby their most memorable image also happens to be a massive spoiler. While this happens because the film has accomplished the rare achievement of breaking through to public consciousness, it also means that future generations aren't surprised by the Statue of Liberty's cameo at the end of *Planet of the Apes* because it's on the DVD cover, and they anticipate John Hurt's disappointing breakfast in *Alien* as it's been referenced for their entire life. By becoming a classic, a film can lose the startling qualities that made it a classic to begin with.

The *Wicker Man*, admittedly, does imply something about its ending with its title, but the eponymous structure's grim arrival isn't the shock it would have been in 1973. Fortunately, the film is more than an unforgettable ending: it's also a landmark in Britain's long tradition of folk horror; a riot of sex and pagan rituals which are disquieting because they seem so out of time. We see Summerisle through the eyes of a repressed outsider; the virginal Christian policeman Neil Howie (Edward Woodward). His prim outrage brings humor, but also leads us towards *that ending* and Woodward's appointment with the Wicker Man. What happens to him isn't a violent act but something more sinister: a trap he unknowingly builds for himself and walks directly into. Even when you know the ending, it still feels like the perfect perverse joke.

It's likely that if you were to walk into the Green Man Inn and ask for a Manhattan—or indeed anything other than a cider made from Summerisle apples—the patrons would fall silent, as they do upon Sergeant Howie's first entrance, but that shouldn't dissuade you from this timeless cocktail.

2 oz. rye whiskey
1 oz. sweet red vermouth
2 dashes of Angostura bitters
1 maraschino cherry, to garnish

1 Add all liquid ingredients into a mixing glass filled with ice cubes.

2 Stir gently but well.

3 Strain into a chilled cocktail glass.

4 Garnish with a maraschino cherry on a toothpick.

THE KARLOFF
Old-Fashioned

BRIDE OF FRANKENSTEIN 1935 DIRECTED BY JAMES WHALE STARRING BORIS KARLOFF, COLIN CLIVE, VALERIE HOBSON

There aren't enough question marks in modern cinema. The glyph has a long history in gimmick-driven credits, from movies finishing with "The End?" to the first appearance of Bond villain, Blofeld in *From Russia with Love*, being credited to "?". But the best-known example comes from James Whale's 1931 version of *Frankenstein*, where the Monster was credited simply as "?".

Following this idea through to its glorious conclusion, it suggests the filmmakers honestly didn't know who played the Monster, and that some undead creature just stumbled onto the set one day. Unamused by this was the actor in question, Boris Karloff, who became a worldwide star in the film's wake. Perhaps in reaction to his early snubbing, by the time he made the sequel *Bride of Frankenstein*, his credit simply read: "KARLOFF."

Of course, dozens of actors have portrayed Mary Shelley's wretched creature, but the definitive image remains that of Boris Karloff: the ragged suit, square forehead, heavily lidded eyes, and bolt through the neck; Frankenstein's power comes from the sympathy Karloff generated for him as a misunderstood figure oddly vulnerable despite his strength, and only driven to anger out of confusion and fear.

Karloff, who played another of Universal's iconic monsters, the Mummy, was one of horror's biggest stars and while the genre's appeal waned as the world grappled with larger horrors, his popularity endured.

1 sugar cube	1 Place sugar cube in an old-fashioned glass.
2 dashes of Angostura Bitters	2 Add a few dashes of the bitters.
2 dashes of water or club soda	3 Add a few dashes of water or club soda.
1 ½ oz. Bourbon	
maraschino cherry, to garnish	4 Muddle until the sugar has dissolved.
orange peel, to garnish	5 Add a few ice cubes.
	6 Add the Bourbon and gently stir.
	7 Garnish with a cherry and a twist of orange peel.

PUTTING OUT FIRE WITH GASOLINE!
Blue Blazer

Val Lewton's 1940s RKO productions relied on tension for budgetary reasons rather than principle, but it proved effective, reducing horror to its fundamentals: an unseen danger, unrealized. In *Cat People*'s most influential scene, Alice (Jane Randolph) walks alone at night through sparse pools of streetlight. The only sound is her high heels, soon joined by a second pair following behind. She spots something but a bus arrives, its brakes sounding just like a panther. We don't need to see what Alice does to fear it.

As the epitome of suggestive horror, *Cat People* was an unusual choice for a 1980s remake, and especially by the screenwriter of *Taxi Driver*. Paul Schrader's version is sultrier by default: even Giorgio Moroder's theme is built around David Bowie wailing, "I've been putting out fire ... with gasoline!"

2 oz. whiskey

2 oz. boiling water

1 ½ tsp. powdered (confectioner's) sugar

twist of lemon, to garnish

Note: stand on a non-flammable floor and have a fire extinguisher to hand. Also, don't actually make this one ... have you lost your mind? If you do try it and burn down your kitchen, please don't tell the firefighters that you were inspired by a book of horror-themed cocktail recipes.

1 Preheat two silver-plated tankards with handles by filling them with boiling water.

2 Slightly warm the whiskey in a saucepan.

3 Discard the boiling water from the tankards.

4 Pour the whiskey into one tankard and 2 oz. boiling water into the other.

5 Using a long match, ignite the whiskey.

6 While it's still blazing, pour the whiskey into the other tankard. Mix the ingredients by pouring the drink between tankards.

7 Extinguish the flame by covering the flaming tankard with the base of the other one.

8 Pour the drink into a brandy balloon glass, stir in powdered sugar, and garnish.

SALTY DOG
Salty Dog

As the most successful and prolific horror writer of the 20th century, more of Stephen King's work has been adapted for film and television than that of any of his peers. It's a mixed blessing: King's unabashed love of schlock puts him in a curious position where some of his books have sold millions of copies, yet their adaptations come across like cheap B-movies. Without King's grounded Maine humor and deceptively light touch, on screen it's all just a bit silly.

Accordingly, many of the strongest King adaptations have come from books that strayed from horror, like *The Shawshank Redemption* or *Stand By Me*, while the one that's seen as a masterpiece, *The Shining*, he famously disowned (understandably but incorrectly) because it diverged from the book, preferring a made-for-TV miniseries version that was more faithful and less ambitious.

And then there's *Cujo*.

Written at the height of King's addiction problems, *Cujo* is the one book of his career that he says he can't remember writing: "I don't say that with pride or shame, only with a vague sense of sorrow and loss. I like that book. I wish I could remember enjoying the good parts as I put them down on the page." Presumably those good parts include its enticing premise: a mother and child trapped in a car by a rabid St. Bernard dog.

Translated to film, this could have become a spartan thriller without an ounce of fat—if made by a filmmaker with a lethal command of tension. It was not.

CUJO 1983 DIRECTED BY LEWIS TEAGUE STARRING DEE WALLACE, DANIEL HUGH KELLY, DANNY PINTAURO

Ingredients		Instructions
lime wedge		1 Rub the lime wedge around the rim of an old-fashioned glass.
coarse salt		2 Dust the rim with coarse salt.
1 ½ oz. gin or vodka		3 Fill the glass with ice.
3 ½ oz. grapefruit juice		4 Add the gin or vodka.
		5 Top with the grapefruit juice and stir gently.

WOULDST THOU LIKE TO LIVE DELICIOUSLY?

Hot Buttered Rum

THE WITCH 2015 DIRECTED BY ROBERT EGGERS STARRING ANYA TAYLOR-JOY, RALPH INESON, KATE DICKIE

It's not a great sign when *The Pilgrims* banish you for being too devout. *The Witch* opens with a family of settlers leaving their New England plantation to build a farm at the edge of a forest and uncolonized America itself. But what lives in that forest?

A folktale featuring arcane dialogue and inspired by historical accounts of alleged witchcraft, *The Witch* was perceived as muted and austere, yet writer-director Robert Eggers finds a conclusion more radical than its flashier peers. Hysteria descends upon William (Ralph Ineson) and Katherine (Kate Dickie) as an inexplicable tragedy is followed by several more. Suspicious of their daughter Thomasin's (Anya Taylor-Joy) nascent sexuality, it's assumed she's made a covenant with the devil and is the cause of the family's suffering. Everything falls apart and Thomasin is left alone in the ruins of their life.

At this point, narrative convention suggests the protagonist will stand up for her family's honor, but instead, something extraordinary happens; a billy goat called Black Phillip transmogrifies into the mortal form of Satan and makes an irrefutable proposal: "Wouldst thou like the taste of butter? A pretty dress? Wouldst thou like to live deliciously?" Thomasin understands that being a witch represents pleasure, which represents freedom—from family, from religion, from a creed asserting that one's very existence is meant to be miserable. After her short, trudging life of servitude, there's only one rational answer.

pinch of cinnamon	1 Add the spices, vanilla, brown sugar, and butter to the bottom of an Irish coffee glass.
pinch of nutmeg	
pinch of allspice	2 Mix well.
splash of vanilla extract	3 Add the rum.
1 tsp. brown sugar	4 Top with the hot water.
1 tbsp. butter, softened	5 Stir until the butter melts.
2 oz. dark rum	
5 oz. hot water	

A NOISY COCKTAIL FOR A QUIET PLACE
"Pop Rocks" Cosmopolitan

A QUIET PLACE 2018 DIRECTED BY JOHN KRASINSKI STARRING EMILY BLUNT, JOHN KRASINSKI, MILLICENT SIMMONDS

Some of the greatest horror films unsettle because of the ambiguities at their outer edges, looming like unidentified shadows in the corner of a darkened bedroom. Who's the Thing at the end of *The Thing*? Are they still being followed at the end of *It Follows*? What's up with that lusty bear man in *The Shining*? It's the mysteries that stick with us, not the answers.

A Quiet Place, by contrast, is relatively tidy, and yet the audience comes away with almost as many questions. Why couldn't the Abbott family have just lived by the waterfall? How come no one else on Earth figured out that aliens with hypersensitive hearing might be vulnerable to high frequencies? Why didn't they wear socks all the time? Such nagging concerns dampen what's an otherwise unfussy horror exercise, as Emily Blunt and John Krasinski attempt to survive the Apocalypse by using their quieter "indoor" voices.

Given their uneven strategies—which somehow include living in a cornfield and leaving glass objects lying around—it's surprising that the film doesn't include a sequence where they make this cocktail and belt out "Total Eclipse of the Heart" at the karaoke mic. That said, do feel free to try this yourself.

A packet of popping candy (strawberry or watermelon)

1 lime wedge

1 tbsp. lime juice

1 ½ oz. vodka

1 oz. unsweetened pomegranate juice

½ oz. Cointreau

1 Lay the popping candy between sheets of parchment paper and lightly crush with a rolling pin.

2 Moisten the rim of a martini glass with the lime wedge then dip the rim into the candy.

3 Fill a cocktail shaker with ice.

4 Add all liquid ingredients and shake well.

5 Strain the drink into the glass.

TRICK OR TREAT
Pumpkin Mule

HALLOWEEN 1978 DIRECTED BY JOHN CARPENTER STARRING DONALD PLEASENCE, JAMIE LEE CURTIS, NICK CASTLE

Horror has never been afraid of repeating itself if there's money to be made, and almost every genre embraced gritty reboots after the 2005 release of *Batman Begins* (although it was technically predated by the remake of *The Texas Chainsaw Massacre*). The following decade saw unnecessary remakes of classics including *A Nightmare on Elm Street*, *Friday the 13th*, *The Evil Dead*, *The Omen*, *The Amityville Horror*, and *The Thing*. The results were uniformly disappointing: dour and humorless, with muted color palettes, practical effects traded out for CGI, and the weird edges sanded away. They were more gory but less scary, failing to recapture the twisted magic of their originals.

It was inevitable that *Halloween* would appear among these reboots. *Halloween* has been remaking itself since it was first released, with its continuity becoming increasingly convoluted, splitting off in three separate directions before you even include the 2007 film and its sequel, or *Halloween III: Season of the Witch*, which doesn't feature Michael Myers and has nothing to do with any other film in the series. The 2007 *Halloween* is a remake of the original 1978 *Halloween*, while the 2019 reboot, also called *Halloween*, is a direct sequel to 1978 *Halloween* and is essentially a remake of 1998's *Halloween H20*.

The unkillable monster is *Halloween*, not Michael Myers. No matter what decade it is, Michael is coming home to Haddonfield for the holidays. Of course, it helps that he's somehow always traveling between sanatoriums in late October, ready to escape. Although the films don't go into it, one thing "The Shape" is likely to find outside his institution is the autumnal prevalence of pumpkin-flavored drinks, including this seasonal mule.

1 oz. pumpkin spice syrup	1 Add the syrup, vodka, and fresh lime juice to a cocktail shaker.
1 ½ oz. vodka	
½ oz. lime juice	2 Shake vigorously.
ginger beer	3 Strain into a highball glass (or a copper mule mug if you have it).
1 cinnamon stick, to garnish	4 Top with ginger beer.
	5 Garnish with a cinnamon stick.

LENORE'S LAMENT
Blackthorn

Of course, it would be a raven. Corvids have been a bad omen for many cultures since antiquity; seen as tricksters or associated with death. No animal is actually evil, but people have always seemed to ignore this logic when it comes to crows, rooks, and ravens. Their crime is that they happen to have ominous black plumage, some feed on carrion, and they are very, very smart: most animals are only as intelligent as they need to be to survive, but members of the crow family are smarter. They can remember people, they get bored, they can manipulate tools. They can learn! So, when Edgar Allan Poe was conceiving of a creature to harass a bereaved lover and tip them into madness, who else would he have tapping at the chamber door but a ghastly grim and ancient raven, wandering from the nightly shore?

Written in trochaic octameter—an unusual meter that's also a pleasure to read aloud, bobbing along mesmerically—the poem made Poe's career, becoming so popular that he was subsequently referred to as *The Raven*. The musicality of the text ensured that it could be easily parodied, a fitting consequence for a poem that is itself dense with literary allusion. It lingers however because it has an unsettling quality that reflects its subject. As the unnamed protagonist concludes his tale, he reveals with his final verse that he hasn't been talking in the past tense. He is trapped: "And the Raven, never flitting, still is sitting, *still* is sitting, On the pallid bust of Pallas just above my chamber door."

2 ½ oz. Irish whiskey		1 Add the whiskey, vermouth, Pernod, and bitters into a cocktail shaker filled with ice.
½ oz. dry vermouth		
2 dashes of Pernod		2 Shake well.
2 dashes of Angostura bitters		3 Strain into a chilled cocktail glass.
lemon peel, to garnish		4 Garnish with the lemon peel.

DEATH IN VENICE
Death in Venice

DON'T LOOK NOW 1973 DIRECTED BY NICOLAS ROEG STARRING JULIE CHRISTIE, DONALD SUTHERLAND, HILARY MASON

The tourist off-season has always been a particularly ripe setting for filmmakers telling stories about anguished protagonists. Jack Torrance's plunge into madness in *The Shining* owes as much to the weather and solitude as to the Overlook Hotel and its many phantasms, while Nicolas Roeg's sublime *Don't Look Now* sees Laura (Julie Christie) and John (Donald Sutherland) stumble around a deserted, echoing Venice, lost in grief. Faced with an unimaginable loss, Laura turns to faith in the supernatural, while John is comforted by scepticism of that same faith. As they disintegrate emotionally in a city that's slightly out of step, the paranormal seems logical in a way it wouldn't have in their normal life. Their grief makes a space for it, but then something unholy takes over that space.

When a film is famous for a twist ending, it's often because that ending dramatically recontextualizes everything we've previously seen. Suddenly, the audience realizes that a character had different motivations the entire time, or a piece of crucial information was actually inverted. This technically happens in *Don't Look Now*, where premonitions are seen in a new light, but the twist, when it comes, is dreadful and strange and uncanny. It feels inevitable not because of breadcrumbs laid through the narrative, but because what happens is so horrible and unexpected that of course it's inevitable. The true horror in *Don't Look Now* is bereavement, and its events are a psychic manifestation of that.

This modern cocktail is named after a Thomas Mann novella, but if he hadn't gotten there first then *Death in Venice* would have been a perfect name for Daphne du Maurier's original short story. It is, at least, an appropriate name for this drink.

½ oz. Campari	1 Pour the Campari and bitters into a chilled flute glass.
2 dashes of grapefruit bitters	
Prosecco	2 Top with Prosecco.

(A HAIRY NAVEL IS) THE LEAST OF HIS PROBLEMS

Hairy Navel

THE WOLF MAN 1941 DIRECTED BY GEORGE WAGGNER STARRING CLAUDE RAINS, WARREN WILLIAM, LON CHANEY JR.

Drawing from both medieval folklore and Gothic fiction like Robert Louis Stevenson's *Strange Case of Dr. Jekyll and Mr. Hyde*, werewolves provide fertile material for movies about transformation or the divided self: in *Ginger Snaps*, lycanthropy is a metaphor for puberty, with its bodily changes, unexpected hair growth and attendant shame. Generally, however, werewolves are an underused resource compared to their supernatural peers.

Special effects are the real werewolf's curse, not the full moon. The compelling part of any werewolf story isn't a hirsute beast indiscriminately slaying townsfolk but that juicy scene where something primal and hidden emerges from an otherwise ordinary person. The problem is that the first werewolf films were unable to convincingly portray the transformation and so would avoid the really good stuff— *The Wolf Man* only shows Lon Chaney Jr.'s feet changing, while later entries in the series could merely offer stiff-looking lap dissolves.

By the time special effects caught up, filmmakers were overly distracted by the "werewolfness" of it all, and the transformation became the whole point. But maybe that's okay. *The Howling*, arriving in the same crowded year as *An American Werewolf in London,* and *Wolfen*, doesn't have any aspirations beyond being fun, yet still disconcerts in the way Robert Picardo's skin pulsates, an interminable throb that augurs the monster hatching violently into life.

1 ½ oz. vodka	1	Add the vodka, peach schnapps, and orange juice to a cocktail shaker filled with ice.
1 oz. peach schnapps		
3 ½ oz. orange juice	2	Stir (don't shake).
slice of orange, to garnish	3	Strain into a highball glass, filled with ice.
	4	Garnish with the orange slice.

A NICE DIP
IN THE OCEAN
Sea Breeze

JAWS 1975 DIRECTED BY STEVEN SPIELBERG STARRING ROY SCHEIDER, ROBERT SHAW, RICHARD DREYFUSS

The best thing that ever happened to Steven Spielberg was his mechanical shark malfunctioning. At this point, *Jaws'* troubled production is mythical—a 27-year-old with a mutinous crew running three months behind schedule who ends up making the highest-grossing film of all time and inventing the summer blockbuster—but it's still a persuasive illustration of how limitations can be creatively valuable.

Burdened with an unreliable shark in his shark movie, Spielberg concentrated instead on suspense and sudden shocks. Until the very climax, the shark is talked about but rarely seen. It doesn't even fully surface for the first 80 minutes. By the time we do get a good look we're primed both to fear it and to accept its reality, and this has worked to age the film better than many blockbusters produced decades later.

Spielberg's youthful hubris made him insist, imprudently, that the film be shot in the actual ocean, rather than a tank; and while this created endless production issues, it also meant that the shark, hidden underwater, felt like a genuine threat at all times. Who needs to see your monster when you can have a grizzled shark hunter say, "You know the thing about a shark, he's got lifeless eyes. Black eyes, like a doll's eyes. When he comes at you, he doesn't seem to be livin' until he bites you, and those black eyes roll over white, and then you hear that terrible high-pitched screaming, and the ocean turns red ..."

It's common for cocktails to emerge organically thanks to an innovative bartender or the replacement of an unavailable key ingredient, but the Sea Breeze's prevalence is probably more a result of the company Ocean Breeze's desire for a popular cranberry juice–based cocktail. Even so, it's a decent summer cocktail for sitting on a beach and not going anywhere near the water whatsoever.

1 ⅓ oz. vodka	1 Fill a highball glass with ice.
4 oz. cranberry juice	2 Add all liquid ingredients.
1 oz. pink grapefruit juice	3 Stir briefly.
lime wedge, to garnish	4 Garnish with the lime wedge.

96

THE INVISIBLE DRINK
Elderflower Gin & Tonic

STARRING ELISABETH MOSS, OLIVER JACKSON-COHEN, HARRIET DYER

THE INVISIBLE MAN 2020 DIRECTED BY LEIGH WHANNELL

Universal has cinema's greatest monsters stuffed into a closet and little idea about what to do with any of them. Since the success of *The Mummy* in 1999, their go-to move has been to squeeze the characters into blockbusters, like the embarrassing attempt to make them superheroes in a Marvel-style "Dark Universe." When this failed, the studio finally decided to get a talented horror filmmaker to direct an actual horror film, who made it relevant by asking the only crucial question: if it was possible to become invisible, who would be the worst person to have that ability?

The answer, regrettably, is an abusive, controlling husband. In Leigh Whannell's *The Invisible Man*, Cecilia (Elisabeth Moss) uses her ingenuity to finally escape her monstrous partner Adrian (Oliver Jackson-Cohen), only to learn after his apparent suicide that he's still alive and has completed his life's work: namely an optical bodysuit that makes him invisible; and that he intends to use it to terrorize her.

Until the bombastic climax, Whannell's approach is defined by restraint, finding the terror in empty hallways and unoccupied chairs. The framing is impeccable: there are always dead spaces around Cecilia where you fear Adrian is hiding.

Moss, as she did in *The Handmaid's Tale*, is able to find many shades within abuse, creating a character who can be brave, shrewd, and deeply frightened in the same moment. Adrian's domestic violence repeats itself not just through his invisible stalking, but by carefully ensuring that no one will believe her. *The Invisible Man*'s true accomplishment isn't finding a new way to depict a classic monster but finding a new way to depict a real-life horror.

2 oz. gin	1 Fill an old-fashioned glass with ice.
1 oz. Elderflower liqueur	2 Add the gin and elderflower liqueur.
1 lime wedge	3 Squeeze the lime wedge into the glass.
tonic water	4 Top with tonic water.
	5 Stir gently.

Shawn:
Lyndsi:

HEAVY WEATHER
Dark 'n' Stormy

In the movies, bad things happen in bad weather: a rainstorm forces you to get off the road and check into a motel, or a blizzard traps you with your murderous husband, a shape-shifting alien, vampires, a murderous fan or Nazi zombies, preventing both escape and rescue.

Weather has always been integral to horror films, typically as atmosphere. Dracula's castle wouldn't be intimidating on a sunny day. It's primal: horror pools in darkness, in the cold and the wet, in conditions where you can't see who, or *what*, is out there.

The weather itself is usually not the threat, but two years after playing an essential role in the development of the slasher genre with *Halloween*, John Carpenter's follow-up was a film where his slow, silent killer was now intangible: a glowing fog, filled with the ghosts of vengeful sailors. This lost the immediacy of Michael Myers, a figure that can be in your house, standing right behind you, but also gave the film the quality of a classic ghost story that its opening campfire scene establishes.

Inclement weather demands an appropriately inclement drink. Gosling's Rum owns the trademark to the name of this cocktail and police it strenuously, so if you use a different dark rum, expect the ghost of 19th century merchant James Gosling to show up shrouded in fog and ready to sue you.

THE FOG 1980 DIRECTED BY JOHN CARPENTER STARRING ADRIENNE BARBEAU, JAMIE LEE CURTIS, JANET LEIGH

3 ⅓ oz. ginger beer	1 Pour the ginger beer into a highball glass filled with ice.
2 oz. Gosling's Rum	2 Top with the rum.
lime wedge, to garnish	3 Squeeze in lime wedge and use as a garnish.

CANDYMAN, CANDYMAN
Jelly Bean

CANDYMAN 1992 DIRECTED BY BERNARD ROSE STARRING VIRGINIA MADSEN, XANDER BERKELEY, TONY TODD

We understand that horror folklore is fictional but also accept its convoluted specifics as if they were historical fact. Of course, you need a silver bullet to kill a werewolf or a wooden stake to dispatch a vampire—everybody knows those are the rules. It's difficult to create a new myth that can convey the same mysterious plausibility when it's only just been conceived. *Candyman*, adapted from Clive Barker's England-set short story *The Forbidden*, achieves the impression of a convincing urban legend: a ghost who can be summoned by repeating his name in a mirror, and will kill you with a hook jammed in his bloody stump.

What makes the story resonant is the tragic biography of its villain: Daniel Robitaille (Tony Todd), son of a slave who made a fortune from mass producing shoes, was a talented artist raised in white society until his interracial relationship was discovered. After the hand he used for painting was removed with a rusty blade, he was smeared with honey and stung to death by bees, and now *Candyman* haunts the Cabrini-Green housing projects where his ashes were scattered.

Although diminishing sequels followed, the Candyman was treated reverently by Todd. Understanding the mythic value of his historically persecuted villain, he refused to make a bizarre crossover with *Leprechaun*, the horror-comedy series about a murderous leprechaun whose pot of gold is usually being stolen. Todd's restraint bore fruit: continuing the modern vogue for rebooting a horror franchise by creating a direct sequel to the original and pretending the other sequels never existed, a new *Candyman* set to release in 2021, is directed by Nia DaCosta and cowritten by Jordan Peele, the writer–director behind *Get Out*.

½ oz. blue Curaçao	
1 ½ oz. pineapple juice	
1 oz. cherry vodka	

1   Pour the blue Curaçao into a tall shot glass.

2   Gently layer the pineapple juice on top of the Curaçao by pouring it over a barspoon.

3   Using the same technique, layer the cherry vodka on top of the pineapple juice.

LET THE RIGHT RUM IN
Mai Tai

STARRING KÅRE HEDEBRANT, LINA LEANDERSSON, PER RAGNAR

Just as romantic comedies tend to focus on the tumultuous, maddening euphoria of courtship rather than the less dramatic relationship that follows, vampire movies often concentrate on the flashy parts of being undead, instead of the long slog of immortality.

Let the Right One In is about the relationship between two youths on the cusp of adolescence, except one of them will never reach it. The connection between eternally-12-years-old vampire Eli (Lina Leandersson) and their young suitor Oskar (Kåre Hedebrant) is genuinely tender but suggests something disquieting when we stop to consider Håkan (Per Ragnar), the old man who cares for Eli. Was he once a lonely boy too, captivated by his mysterious neighbor? Will Oskar be brought into immortality or will he also end up as a serial killer to satisfy Eli's unholy thirst, until they eventually forget him and meets another lonely boy?

In recent years the vampire/familiar dynamic has been played mostly for laughs in the film and television versions of *What We Do in the Shadows*, but the reality of such a one-sided relationship is heartbreaking. Eli does love Oskar, but vampirism, at its heart, isn't about the draining of blood from strangers but the siphoning of something from a person for their entire life. We view a romance as tragic when death or circumstances tear a couple apart; in *Let the Right One In*, the tragedy is that they might stay together.

LET THE RIGHT ONE IN 2008 DIRECTED BY TOMAS ALFREDSON

1 oz. light rum	1	Add all liquid ingredients except the dark rum into a cocktail shaker filled with ice.
½ oz. orange Curaçao		
½ oz. Orgeat syrup	2	Shake well for around 10–15 seconds until a frost forms on the outside of the shaker.
½ oz. lime juice		
¼ oz. simple syrup		
1 oz. dark rum	3	Strain into an old-fashioned glass, containing a few ice cubes.
maraschino cherry, to garnish	4	Top off with the dark rum, using a barspoon so it'll spread evenly.
slice of lime, to garnish		
sprig of mint, to garnish	5	Garnish with the cherry, lime slice, and mint sprig.

GUESS WHO'S HERE
Black Jack

THE BABADOOK 2014 DIRECTED BY JENNIFER KENT STARRING ESSIE DAVIS, NOAH WISEMAN, DANIEL HENSHALL

A strange pop-up book materializes in the home of Amelia (Essie Davis) and her son Samuel (Noah Wiseman), threatening the arrival of "Mister Babadook" and filled with blank pages. While coping with her son's emotional difficulties and his obsessive fear of invisible monsters, as well as her own unresolved grief about her husband's death, Amelia is slowly terrorized by phenomena that can be explained away, making her look mad to outsiders. Like *The Shining* transported to a small Australian home, the Babadook unlocks Amelia's violent resentment and she turns from victim to villain, flailing between abuse and apologies, terrified that she's going to do something terrible to the son.

It's apt that Mister Babadook emerges from the pages of a children's book, as his appearance—top hat, slender fingers, pinprick eyes, and blackened mouth—feels like some unchallenged derangement from an archaic nursery rhyme, or else a terrifying figure from a silent movie glimpsed late at night. He seemingly represents both taboo parental frustration and the trauma of grief. The pop-up book's troubling promise, "If it's in a word or it's in a look, you can't get rid of the Babadook" comes to mean something deeper: grief isn't something to be defeated and forgotten about, but becomes part of the texture of one's life.

With its shifting reality, cathartic narrative, and intense mother–son relationship, writer–director Jennifer Kent imbued *The Babadook* with a subtextual richness that invites competing interpretations: Mister Babadook made his most surprising move not during the events of the film but afterwards, becoming an unlikely LGBTQIA+ symbol. Initially arising out of an absurd meme, this development was nevertheless wryly embraced by the community and took on a life of its own, prompting queer interpretations of the film, both irreverent and sincere.

1 ½ oz. cherry brandy	1 Add all ingredients into a cocktail shaker, filled with ice.
⅓ oz. Cognac	2 Shake well.
1 ½ oz. cold coffee	3 Strain into a martini glass.
½ oz. simple syrup	

RECKLESS 80S TEENAGER
Sex on the Beach

FRIDAY THE 13TH 1980 DIRECTED BY SEAN S. CUNNINGHAM STARRING ADRIENNE KING, BETSY PALMER, JEANNINE TAYLOR

Friday the 13th follows, lumbering, in the footsteps of Michael Myers. A transparent attempt to cash in on *Halloween*'s popularity two years earlier, it presented another plodding teen-killer tied to a spooky date. Without an original thought in its head, the most interesting thing about the original film is the ultimate identity of the villain, but that twist was immediately forgotten for the many, many sequels.

The series is a strange brew, attaining cultural significance from the exhausting number of installments rather than qualities possessed by any individual outing. Jason Voorhees himself doesn't become the killer until the second film and doesn't get his famous hockey mask until the third. His corpse is hit by lightning and he becomes a zombie in the sixth; visits New York for some reason in the eighth, fights Freddy Krueger in the eleventh, and somehow goes to space at one point. He'll be whatever you want him to be if you'll just buy a ticket.

Denouncing teenage sexuality, while simultaneously leering over it, *Friday the 13th* shows how successful a horror franchise can be with a good mask and a memorable theme tune, and also how you could get away with just about anything in the 1980s. Speaking of which: the main ingredients of Sex on the Beach are peach schnapps, vodka, melted Rubik's Cubes, a Wham! cassingle, and orange juice. The drink is emblematic of the simple fruity cocktails that became popular in the decade, each containing as much vodka as the glass's volume would allow. These were saddled with risqué names like Screaming Orgasm, Slippery Nipple, and Slow Comfortable Screw Against the Wall. Until irony reclaims it, Sex on the Beach serves as an object lesson that what's provocative today can be tedious tomorrow.

1 ½ oz. vodka	1 Add all liquid ingredients to a cocktail shaker filled with ice.
0.75 oz. peach schnapps	2 Shake vigorously.
1 ½ oz. orange juice	3 Strain into a highball glass filled with ice cubes.
1 ½ oz. cranberry juice	
orange slice, to garnish	4 Garnish with half an orange slice and a cocktail umbrella, if desired.
cocktail umbrella (optional)	

THE HAUNTING OF CHILLED GROUSE
Highland Fling

THE HAUNTING OF HILL HOUSE 2018 CREATED BY MIKE FLANAGAN STARRING MICHIEL HUISMAN, CARLA GUGINO, HENRY THOMAS

Given a glimpse of something terrible, the mind fills in the blanks. This is the first lesson of horror: what you don't see is always scarier than what you do. When the lights are switched on, the murderer turns out to be a coat stand after all. *The Haunting of Hill House* managed to become a phenomenon on Netflix by exploiting this simple idea, stretching out the tension of Shirley Jackson's 1959 novel by keeping you doubting what you've just seen. Was there a face in that window? Did something move in the corner? Is there someone under the piano?

Within the series dozens of ghosts hide in plain sight, or maybe there aren't any at all. Over time, the same ones seem to occur in certain locations, adding an uncomfortable texture to seemingly normal scenes. Given that the audience is able to immediately check, this approach by the series' creator Mick Flanagan is confident, and what makes it even more impressive, that it actually works: when you rewind 10 seconds, pause, and see that—yes!—there *is* a man lurking behind the door, it's somehow much, much worse.

It would be reasonable to want a drink to withstand it all. The location of *Hill House* isn't specified in either the book or the series, and while Scotland wouldn't be the obvious conclusion (none of the characters are Scottish, for one), let's go with it. Scotland isn't especially famous for its cocktails—why would you need to be, when you've been making whiskey since the Middle Ages—but this one is an effective use of blended Scotch.

1 ½ oz. Famous Grouse or another Scotch whiskey	1 Add the whiskey, vermouth, and bitters to a cocktail shaker.
¾ oz. sweet vermouth	2 Shake vigorously.
2 dashes of orange bitters	3 Strain into a chilled cocktail glass.
1 green olive, to garnish	4 Garnish with an olive on a toothpick.

666
Six Cylinder

THE OMEN 1976   DIRECTED BY RICHARD DONNER   STARRING GREGORY PECK, LEE REMICK, DAVID WARNER

It'd be possible to watch America's horror output from the late 1960s to the mid-'70s and conclude that the nation's biggest threat was conspiring Satanists. The devil certainly got around for a few years, fathering children in *Rosemary's Baby* and *The Omen* and popping up as the unseen antagonist of *The Exorcist* (technically the demon Pazuzu). There isn't a single explanation for this trend, but it reflected the "end-of-days" atmosphere that enveloped a country dealing with multiple psychological tensions from the Vietnam War to the murk of the Nixon administration.

Coming last, *The Omen* was a clear attempt to exploit the success of *The Exorcist*, discarding the medical drama and crisis of faith in favor of a poppier version built around elaborate periodic deaths. Without a tangible figure enacting the killings, these set-pieces thrill rather than scare; setting a template for the *Final Destination* series a quarter of a century later. *The Omen* is remembered as being about a child (Harvey Spencer Stephens) who's the Antichrist, but his evil is largely potential energy. When his nanny is hypnotized by a dog, climbing out of a window to hang herself during his 5th birthday party (which is poor form), she shouts, "Look at me, Damien! It's all for you!"

Damien's ambassador father (Gregory Peck) confirms his fate by finding a birthmark in the shape of three sixes, "the number of the beast." This cocktail is similarly marked and named because of its six ingredients in equal quantities. Hopefully this doesn't mean that the drink will rise from the eternal sea and create armies on either shore, as that would put a damper on any cocktail party.

½ oz. gin	1 Add all liquid ingredients to a cocktail shaker filled with ice.
½ oz. cherry brandy	
½ oz. Campari	2 Stir.
½ oz. sweet vermouth	3 Strain into a chilled martini glass.
½ oz. dry vermouth	4 Garnish with a lemon twist.
½ oz. Dubonnet	
lemon twist, to garnish	

BLOW MY SKULL OFF
Blow My Skull Off

EVIL DEAD II 1987 DIRECTED BY SAM RAIMI STARRING BRUCE CAMPBELL, SARAH BERRY, DAN HICKS

The Evil Dead is so appealing because it was created by a bunch of punk kids figuring out filmmaking as they went. This meant, unsurprisingly, that the production was a mess—crew members were frequently injured and slept in the freezing cold, actual cabin used in the film, and writer-director Sam Raimi was under the misguided impression that his actors needed to really be in pain in order to convey it. But this spirited naivety also made the film distinctive. Its informal unprofessionalism compelled Raimi to improvise, inadvertently forming his entire visual aesthetic: to depict the perspective of the unseen evil force, without the money to hire a Steadicam, they instead tied a camera to a two-by-four and got two grips to run with it around the woods. The results were rough, kinetic, and electrifying.

Raimi was lucky too in casting his high school friend Bruce Campbell as the lead Ash Williams. By chance he'd stumbled across the most game actor possible, willing to put up with just about anything if it'd be scary or funny or gross: Campbell has never met a bookcase that he can't get trapped under. While they embraced splatter and gore with youthful zeal, what made *The Evil Dead*, and later its sequel/remake *Evil Dead II*, irresistible was Raimi's love of vaudeville and slapstick. By *Evil Dead II*, students who barely knew what they were doing had become young professionals, and the tone was more manic and funnier: it's arresting enough to have Ash cut off his own possessed hand with a chainsaw, but he then proceeds to trap it under a bucket weighed down with a copy of Hemingway's *A Farewell to Arms*.

Serves 10

2 ¾ cups brown sugar

16 oz. boiling water

juice of 3 limes

8 oz. rum

8 oz. porter or ale

4 oz. brandy

1 In a large bowl, dissolve the brown sugar in the boiling water.

2 Add the lime juice, rum, porter or ale, and brandy.

3 Stir.

4 Refrigerate until chilled.

5 Serve in half-pint glasses.

CLOVERFIELD CLUB
Clover Club

CLOVERFIELD 2008 DIRECTED BY MATT REEVES STARRING MICHAEL STAHL-DAVID, JESSICA LUCAS, LIZZY CAPLAN

Horror assimilates the anxieties of its age and reflects them right back at the audience. The trauma of 9/11 left deep-seated marks throughout popular culture, but lengthy production cycles meant it took several years to be digested by Hollywood.

Both *Cloverfield* and *War of the Worlds* reinterpreted 9/11 as an alien assault, but while Steven Spielberg purposefully filmed his invasion from ground-level, he also diluted his intentions by having Tom Cruise running around in a leather jacket. Screenwriter Drew Goddard and director Matt Reeves, meanwhile, reimagined the attack as a Kaiju-style monster movie, told through the medium that most people had experienced it: shaky camera footage, shot by terrified bystanders. By withholding "Clover" from the view of both the characters and the audience, *Cloverfield* remedied the CGI folly of the last behemoth to strike New York, Roland Emmerich's *Godzilla* in 1998.

The Blair Witch Project was an effective fluke of a format that was so quickly parodied it seemed like a creative brick wall—even its poorly-received sequel eschewed camcorder minimalism for conventional gloss and gore—but within a decade other horror films like *Cloverfield*, *REC,* and *Paranormal Activity* would consciously exploit the potential of found footage. The subgenre would soon become another tired shortcut for unoriginal filmmakers, but when combined with a creature feature and the tinge of an historic tragedy, the outcome is thrilling.

1 ½ oz. gin
½ oz. raspberry syrup or grenadine
½ oz. lemon juice
1 egg white
raspberries, to garnish

1 Add all ingredients (except the raspberries) into a cocktail shaker.

2 Shake vigorously.

3 Add cubed ice to the shaker.

4 Shake again to chill and dilute the drink.

5 Strain into a chilled martini glass.

6 Garnish with fresh raspberries.

THE CABINET OF DR. CALIGARI 1920 DIRECTED BY ROBERT WIENE STARRING WERNER KRAUSS, CONRAD VEIDT, FRIEDRICH FEHER

THE DRINKS CABINET OF DR. CALIGARI

Aunt Roberta

While the underlying themes of horror—myths about the dark, the strange, the sinister—are ancient, the means of depicting them on film are relatively new compared to other art forms. An entire cinematic language has developed over the medium's short history, exploiting cinematography and editing (and later sound) so that films could move beyond the merely unsettling and instead actively frighten audiences. To watch horror-related silent films is to witness the birth of such techniques before your eyes. They aren't straightforwardly scary but, with careful attention paid, the lack of dialogue has an eerie effect: unexpected and unexplained imagery takes on a dream logic that can't fully exist when characters are able to articulate what's going on.

The Cabinet of Dr. Caligari processed the churning devastation of World War I that had only ended two years earlier, influencing a century of horror and becoming the archetypal example of German Expressionism. Its jagged, tortured sets have a vivid artificiality—even the shadows are painted—that attains emotional authenticity. Both the world and the characters who inhabit it are at a wrong angle: decades later, its story of hypnotist Dr. Caligari (Werner Krauss) using the somnambulist Cesare (Conrad Veidt) to murder would be reevaluated as an unheeded warning about a country vulnerable to the authority of a tyrant.

Dr. Caligari would have to raid his undoubtedly askew drinks cabinet to make an Aunt Roberta, which is possibly the world's strongest cocktail, and is certainly the strongest cocktail in this book. The *entirety* of its ingredients are four spirits and a liqueur—no mixers, no fruit, nowhere to hide—so do take care with this one.

⅓ oz. brandy	1 Pour all ingredients into a cocktail shaker filled with ice.
1 oz. vodka	
⅔ oz. absinthe	2 Shake well.
½ oz. gin	3 Strain into a chilled cocktail glass.
⅓ oz. blackberry liqueur	

THE
SNACKS

NIGHT OF THE LIVING CHEDDAR PASTRY BITES
Olive and cheese bites

NIGHT OF THE LIVING DEAD 1968 DIRECTED BY GEORGE A. ROMERO STARRING DUANE JONES, JUDITH O'DEA, KARL HARDMAN

Zombies are as scary as any other monster, but they aren't actually evil. There's something pathetic and deeply sad about a trapped one, feebly gnashing away for reasons it doesn't understand. Their first non-voodoo outing was in *Night of the Living Dead*, and it's remarkable how the formula was already complete by 1968: disparate survivors trapped in a location, and the group's most abrasive member inevitably leads to the death of almost everyone else. Elaborate zombie gore would come later, but the white faces and smoky eyeshadow are more alarming: "ghouls" tottering out of the darkness in stark black-and-white. They don't look like our modern conception of zombies, they just look like people.

Night of the Living Dead's long influence is thanks in part to its copyright history: as the theatrical distributor didn't place a copyright notice on the title card, it fell instantly into the public domain. This denied director George A. Romero a small fortune, but essentially brought zombies into the public domain too, joining longer-established supernatural creatures as "fair game." While Romero progressively cast Duane Jones as the African American protagonist Ben, the depiction of Barbara (Judith O'Dea) is disappointing, with her shock at the zombie outbreak instantly rendering her completely mute.

Despite this stumble, the film offers one of cinema's bleakest endings. After surviving an inconceivable, unnatural plague through his quick thinking and decisive heroism, Ben is shot dead by a white police officer quick to assume he's just another ghoul. Over the credits, his body is dragged with metal hooks and thrown on a bonfire. *Night of the Living Dead* moved horror beyond the Gothic and into the real world and would beget half a century of zombie fiction, but nothing that followed in its lurching footsteps would be as devastating. It's an ending that, tragically, has never stopped being relevant.

Makes 20 pastry bites

6 oz. cheddar cheese, grated

3 oz. all-purpose flour

½ oz. butter, plus 1 tbsp. for greasing

1 tsp. paprika

½ tsp. ground mustard

20 pimento-stuffed green olives

cayenne pepper, to sprinkle

1 Preheat oven to 400°F.

2 In a food processor, mix the cheese, flour, butter, paprika, and ground mustard until the mixture resembles breadcrumbs.

3 Wrap thumb-sized pieces of the dough around each olive, pressing to make it stick. You will probably need to brush each olive with a little water.

4 Add the coated olives to a greased baking tray and bake for 15 minutes or until the pastry is golden.

5 Remove the olives from the baking tray and sprinkle with cayenne pepper.

6 Serve warm or cold.

PARANORMAL EGGTIVITY
Deviled Eggs

PARANORMAL ACTIVITY 2007 DIRECTED BY OREN PELI STARRING KATIE FEATHERSTON, MICAH SLOAT, MARK FREDRICHS

Space operas and fantasy epics benefit from huge budgets, which allow them the special effects and set design needed to portray elaborate environments. Horror works in reverse: it's rare to find a big-budget horror movie that's actually any good. The genre is intrinsically transgressive, trafficking in violence and the grotesque. It thrives in the unpolished, the dirty and the cheap, which might fool you for a moment into thinking you're watching real-life and not a film: the expensive computer-generated ghosts of 1999's *The Haunting*, for example, can't hope to compete with the scene in *Paranormal Activity* where a woman wakes up suddenly.

Paranormal Activity tests this thesis to the limit. Its budget was only $15,000, which might be just about enough for a new compact car. They don't even spring for a second location, with the film shot entirely in director Oren Peli's actual suburban home. And yet *Paranormal Activity* is effective because the filmmaker had to approach these limitations creatively, creating a sense of dread to make otherwise-mundane things scary.

Nothing happens most of the time, purposefully. It's the anticipation that gets you, the waiting and waiting as Katie (Katie Featherston) and Micah (Micah Sloat) are progressively tormented by an unseen supernatural presence. By returning to the same austere setup—a bed and an open door—again and again, the audience becomes uneasy at its every appearance, and primed to react to its smallest changes. The film understands that the creepiest thing in the world can be an unexpected noise in the middle of the night, or the abrupt, unexplained slam of a door.

Makes 12 deviled eggs

6 eggs

1 oz. mayonnaise

1 tsp. Dijon mustard

salt and pepper

paprika

chives, chopped

1. Hard-boil the eggs in a saucepan.
2. Peel the eggs and cut them in half lengthwise.
3. Remove the yolks with a spoon and place in a bowl, setting aside the egg whites.
4. Mix the yolks, mayonnaise, and mustard with a pinch of salt, pepper, and paprika.
5. Spoon the yolk mixture back into the egg whites.
6. Sprinkle with paprika before topping with chopped chives.

A LITERAL BIRD BOX
Katsu chicken skewers

BIRD BOX 2018 DIRECTED BY SUSANNE BIER STARRING SANDRA BULLOCK, TREVANTE RHODES, JOHN MALKOVICH

What infinitesimal convulsions of the universe must occur to produce two volcano-themed disaster movies in the same year? How did we end up with competing films about neurotic ants, Truman Capote, and asteroids heading for Earth?

Perhaps it's coincidence, or perhaps it's as simple as two studios owning the rights to similar projects, and news of one imminent production prompting the other to race to beat them to market. But ideas tend to emerge organically from different places at the same time, so maybe—like the contested invention of the telephone—it just so happened that in 2011 there were two completely unrelated romantic comedies about friends hooking up.

Such films become twins, forever linked in our imaginations due to their inadvertent proximity, with one deemed the unofficial winner by metrics that are fuzzy and emotional. In 2018, this fate befell *Bird Box* and *A Quiet Place*, two post-apocalyptic horror films about mysterious entities attacking people in a fashion that necessitates limiting a single sense to survive. The characters in *A Quiet Place* must remain unheard, while those in *Bird Box* mustn't look upon their foes, otherwise they'll go mad and take their own lives.

Posterity will decide the eventual "winner," but no one can quite claim to have gotten there first: although *Bird Box* was released nine months later than *A Quiet Place*, it's an adaption of a 2014 novel, while *A Quiet Place* bears some resemblance to the 2015 novel *The Silence*; and the 2019 film adaptation of *The Silence* bears some resemblance to *A Quiet Place*.

All of them are pretty average.

Makes approximately 18 skewers

3 chicken breasts

3 tbsp. soy sauce

juice of 1 lime

3 tbsp. honey

1 tbsp. vegetable oil

1 onion, finely chopped

1 carrot, finely chopped

thumb-size piece of ginger, peeled and grated

3 garlic cloves, crushed

1 tbsp. medium curry powder

½ tsp. ground turmeric

14 fl. oz. can of coconut milk

1 tbsp. all-purpose flour

wooden skewers, soaked in water

1 Preheat oven to 350°F.

2 Slice the chicken into strips and marinate in the soy sauce, lime juice, and 2 tablespoons of honey. Refrigerate.

3 Heat the oil in a large frying pan. Saute the onion and carrot until softened and starting to caramelize.

4 Add the ginger and garlic for 30 seconds then stir in the curry powder and turmeric.

5 Add the coconut milk, 3 ⅓ fl. oz. water and 1 tablespoon of honey.

6 Bring to a boil, reduce the heat and simmer for 15–20 minutes until thickened, adding flour.

7 Remove from the heat and blitz the carrots and onions with a stick blender. Keep dip warm.

8 Skewer each chicken strip individually and place on a baking sheet.

9 Bake for 10–15 minutes until the chicken is cooked through.

10 Serve on a tray with the katsu dip.

127

EXIT STRATEGY
Muffuletta

SAW 2004 DIRECTED BY JAMES WAN STARRING CARY ELWES, LEIGH WHANNELL, DANNY GLOVER

While America contemplated the ethical quagmire of the War on Terror campaign, its horror films lingered on masochism and mutilation. In the early 2000s, the nation just couldn't get torture out of its mind: unrelenting graphic sequences, once the domain of splatter movies and confined to the underground, now appeared in the biggest mainstream hits.

Saw is usually identified as the genesis of "torture porn," but its appeal has as much to do with its intricate, deadly traps as those gory aspects: you can draw a straight line between the franchise and the subsequent rise of escape rooms.

A psychopath chasing someone with a knife is scary, but scarier still is a psychopath with a *plan*. Although the needle pits, knife chairs, and reverse bear traps became increasingly complicated as the films progressed, the basic hook remained: captives forced to commit ironic damage to their own bodies in order to escape contraptions, and the story inevitably ending with a nasty twist in the tale. This allowed *Saw* to endure past the dark national moment of its conception, even though the series—like all profitable horror franchises—would eventually wear out its welcome and outlive the serial killer Jigsaw by five movies.

With its treacherous layers of fillings this Muffuletta-inspired loaf might also seem like some kind of trap, one requiring a sound exit strategy if you're going to eat it without losing half to the floor. However, it's surprisingly easy to construct. Essentially you hollow out a cob and fill it with your favorite things, using as much as you'd like (or at least as much as you can fit in). The components listed here work well, but you can use any ingredients you'd like—they don't have to be fiendishly inspired by the moral failings of your guests.

Serves 6

1 large cob loaf

Gouda

Swiss cheese

roasted red peppers

oil-packed mixed olives, chopped

hummus

pesto

mayonnaise

salami

Italian ham

sundried or cherry tomatoes

lettuce

basil

1 Cut a large circle in the top of the loaf to create a "lid" and remove it.

2 Hollow out the loaf by removing the bread inside.

3 Add the ingredients in layers, seasoning with salt and pepper and drizzling oil every few layers, until you've reached the top.

4 Place the lid back on the loaf.

5 Wrap the loaf in parchment paper and place it in the fridge with something heavy on top.

6 Leave for a few hours or overnight.

7 When ready to eat, slice the loaf into wedges using a sharp serrated knife.

THE (PARTY) RING
Spinach and artichoke bread ring

THE RING 2002 DIRECTED BY GORE VERBINSKI STARRING NAOMI WATTS, MARTIN HENDERSON, BRIAN COX

When is a remake necessary? While certain stories recur, again and again, as new filmmakers bring a perspective from their own era, English-language remakes are motivated by one sole factor: money. In horror, this follows a familiar pattern: something comes along that's exciting and singular and—most uncommonly of all—actually scary. The only problem is that it's made in a foreign language, and so the perfectly weighted *Let the Right One In* becomes the redundant *Let Me In*; and *Ju-on: The Grudge* becomes, well, *The Grudge*, made by the same director. These films, despite everything, are usually pretty good, which is unsurprising when they trace the originals beat for beat except, inevitably, for a few bigger scares.

Most new trends are not new trends at all, but a noteworthy flurry of remakes followed the success of *The Ring*, which managed to match its J-horror progenitor *Ringu*—a good film that admittedly takes a long, long walk to get where it's going. It helps that it starred Naomi Watts, an actress born for horror movies even though she has starred in surprisingly few. The concept is irresistible: there's a video tape and if you watch it you will die exactly seven days later, for reasons unknown, from causes unknown. You do not need to have grown up with physical media to appreciate the proposition. In both versions the contents of the tape—a woman brushing her hair in a mirror, a man with a towel covering his head, a well in a forest—aren't straightforwardly violent or gory (although *The Ring* is trying much harder to be creepy) but there's something slightly off about it all.

The "ring" of the title might represent the call someone receives after watching the cursed videotape, but the characters would've had a much nicer time if it had referred to this bread dip. Be warned, though: after you make it, you will be visited in seven days by a malevolent cheese platter.

Serves 6

12 balls of frozen dinner rolls

8 oz. cream cheese, softened

2 oz. Parmesan cheese, grated

2 oz. Romano cheese, grated

2 ¼ oz. mozzarella cheese, shredded

2 ¼ oz. sour cream

14 oz. artichoke heart, drained and chopped

4 oz. frozen chopped spinach, thawed and drained of excess water

4 cloves garlic, chopped

1 tsp. dried basil

½ tsp. red pepper flakes

olive oil, for coating the skillet and brushing the unbaked rolls

1 Preheat oven to 375°F.

2 Coat a 10-inch, oven-safe skillet with olive oil.

3 Place the dinner roll dough balls in a ring around the edge, cover the skillet with a lid and leave the dough balls to rise until thawed and doubled in size.

4 Add all the other ingredients into a bowl and mix well.

5 Uncover the skillet and scoop the dip into the center.

6 Brush the rolls with olive oil (you can also sprinkle some cheese on them at this point).

7 Place in the oven for 25 minutes.

8 Serve hot while trying to resist watching that cursed videotape you found.

BLACK SUNDAE
Mini Sundaes

BLACK SUNDAY 1960   DIRECTED BY MARIO BAVA   STARRING BARBARA STEELE, JOHN RICHARDSON, ANDREA CHECCHI

"In the 17th century," the narrator tells us, "Satan was abroad on the Earth."

It's the opening scene of *Black Sunday*, and the witch Asa Vajda has been sentenced to death by her brother. *The Mask of Satan* (the film's Italian title, *La Maschera del Demonio*) is brought forward. From Asa's perspective we see the inside: it's covered in spikes. She places a curse on everyone in the name of Satan. It does no good: a hooded executioner uses a mallet to pound the mask into place. Blood pours from its eye sockets. The scene is as disturbing today as it must have been 60 years ago, but something interesting is happening.

The "final girl" taking revenge against their tormentor is now understood as an integral part of horror—a complicated trope (chastity is often a prerequisite) that's inspired decades of insightful feminist film theory. For much of cinema's history, however, female leads were passive damsels to be captured then rescued, expected to offer little except screams and declarations of love.

Horror's evolving attitudes are illustrated by *Black Sunday*, Mario Bava's directorial debut. Barbara Steele plays both Asa and her descendant Katia, a simpering princess wholly dependent upon male instruction. It feels like two eras of cinema sitting within the same film. *Black Sunday* inspired a vibrant wave of Italian horror movies, many starring Steele as scheming, adulterous vixens, driven by forbidden emotions. Of course, these women would inevitably be punished violently for their transgressions, but it was still a kind of breakthrough.

Black Sunday begins with Asa's execution, so we don't know what happened in her final hours, but hopefully they allowed her a last meal, and hopefully mini sundaes existed in 17th century Italy.

Serves 6

3 ½ oz. dark chocolate, broken into chunks

7 fl oz. milk

11 oz. can of caramel

3 oz. crunchy peanut butter

4 oatmeal or peanut butter cookies (without chips), broken into chunks

1 ¾ oz. salted roasted peanuts, roughly chopped

6 scoops of vanilla ice cream

6 scoops of chocolate ice cream

1 Add the chocolate and half the milk to a small saucepan.

2 Add the caramel, peanut butter, and the other half of the milk to a second pan.

3 Gently heat both pans, stirring until thick. Set aside to cool.

4 Stir both sauces to loosen them.

5 Layer both sauces, the cookie chunks, peanuts, and a scoop of each ice cream into six sundae glasses.

28 TRAYS LATER
Millionaire's shortbread traybake

28 DAYS LATER 2002 DIRECTED BY DANNY BOYLE STARRING CILLIAN MURPHY, NAOMIE HARRIS, CHRISTOPHER ECCLESTON

The central idea of zombie fiction is that the living are a much bigger threat than the undead. When things fall apart, as they invariably do, it's the consequence of interpersonal problems and people acting selfishly in their own interests. Zombies, manageable on their own, are only an issue in overwhelming numbers: they're fundamentally a pandemic that can be beaten with collective action and calm, effective coordination. This dynamic lasted for thirty years, until they learned to run ...

Before *28 Days Later*, zombies were generally in no hurry— they were dead, after all. Then director Danny Boyle cast retired athletes as his zombie horde, and instead of a creeping, inescapable plague, they were now a frenzy. They weren't even dead; they just had a rage-inducing virus.

While the film was still concerned with the violence of humans, there was a new immediacy to the danger, exacerbated by the use of digital video and Boyle's typically hyperactive camerawork.

This invigorated the action sequences but turned an existential problem into a physical one: it's hard to blame your demise on the unraveling of social threads if you're killed by a zombie sprinting at you full pelt.

The trend of running zombies survived a little longer, most notably in Zack Snyder's gripping but empty remake of *Dawn of the Dead*, before the television adaptation of *The Walking Dead* overpowered the fences and shuffled into the compound.

Makes 18 squares

For the shortbread

7 oz. butter, softened

3 ½ oz. superfine sugar

3 ½ oz. semolina

7 oz. all-purpose flour

For the caramel

10 oz. butter, diced

5 oz. superfine sugar

2 ⅔ oz. light corn syrup

14 oz. can condensed milk

For the chocolate

10 oz. good-quality dark chocolate

1 Preheat oven to 340°F and butter a Swiss roll tin.

2 Mix the shortbread ingredients until the dough is smooth.

3 Press the dough into the tin and prick it all over with a fork.

4 Bake for 15–20 minutes until golden and firm. Remove from the oven and leave to cool.

5 In a saucepan, stir the caramel ingredients over a low heat until the butter has melted.

6 Simmer gently for 15 minutes, stirring constantly, until the mixture has thickened.

7 Pour over the cold shortbread and leave to cool again.

8 Break up the chocolate before melting it in a heatproof bowl over a pan of simmering water.

9 Pour the chocolate over the cooled caramel layer, spreading it evenly with a palette knife.

10 Refrigerate until set, then cut into squares.

AT THE MOUNTAINS OF MARINARA
Garlic Bread Sticks with Marinara dipping sauce

LOVECRAFT COUNTRY 2020 CREATED BY MISHA GREEN STARRING JURNEE SMOLLETT, JONATHAN MAJORS, COURTNEY B. VANCE

Reconciling someone's personal beliefs with their artistic output can be disorientating, but with H.P. Lovecraft it's impossible to parse the two: his tentacled monstrosities and rancid worldview are inseparable. On a fundamental level, all of his work was about a fear of "the Other." The palpable disgust that Lovecraft drew from to depict shoggoths, sentient mutagenic colors, and colossal worms worshiped by insane death cults is the same source as his racism, bigotry, and white supremacy.

Lovecraft's inexhaustible dedication to cosmic horror—his "Elder Things" aren't deities or supernatural monsters but extraterrestrials from the void; terrifying in their awesome scale and indifferent to us, and so incomprehensible that you lose your mind by looking upon them—was generally ignored during his lifetime, and direct adaptations of his key stories like *At the Mountains of Madness* have often struggled to reach the screen, but Lovecraft's work has profoundly influenced horror from Stephen King to John Carpenter, *Alien* to *Ghostbusters*.

While Lovecraft's racism has been examined critically since his death, writers and filmmakers have been content to pull inspiration from his Eldritch terrors without interrogating the slimy ideology beneath the slimy creatures. It took much longer, most notably in the Matt Ruff's 2016 book *Lovecraft Country* and Misha Green's subsequent television adaptation, for Lovecraft's racism to be properly reflected within Lovecraftian horror.

Makes 8–10 bread sticks

4 oz. extra-virgin olive oil

4 tbsp. unsalted butter

3 large garlic cloves, crushed

1 oz. flatleaf parsley, chopped

1 large baguette, split and halved

1 ½ oz. Pecorino Romano cheese, grated

marinara sauce, for serving

1 Preheat oven to 450°F.

2 In a medium skillet, add the olive oil and melt the butter.

3 Turn up the heat, add the garlic and cook for 1 minute.

4 Remove from the heat and add the parsley.

5 Place the bread on a baking sheet, face up.

6 Spoon the garlic butter on top.

7 Sprinkle with cheese.

8 Bake in the oven for 10 minutes.

9 Place bread under the grill for a minute, until just golden.

10 Cut into ½-inch "fries."

11 Serve in cups alongside a dipping bowl of marinara sauce.

INDEX

THANKS

Thank you to Susan Clark and Kate Pollard for their generosity, skill, and patience during the writing of this book, and to Emma Clifton and my parents for helping keep the ship afloat.

ABOUT
JASON WARD

Jason Ward is a writer and journalist based in Glasgow,
Scotland. He has written about film for publications including
the *Guardian*, *Little White Lies* and *Dazed*, as well as the
books *Movie Star Chronicles* and *1001 Movies You Must
See Before You Die*. He is also the author of books including
Should You Buy This Book? and *Edgar Allan Poe's Puzzles
From Beyond the Grave*. As a child, he once stayed up late to
watch *Night of the Living Dead* and has never gotten over it.

Thunder Bay Press
An imprint of Printers Row Publishing Group
9717 Pacific Heights Blvd, San Diego, CA 92121
www.thunderbaybooks.com • mail@thunderbaybooks.com

Correspondence regarding the content of this book should be sent
to Thunder Bay Press, Editorial Department, at the above address.
Author, illustration, and rights inquiries should be sent to:
Orange Hippo!
20 Mortimer Street
London W1T 3JW
www.welbeckpublishing.com

Thunder Bay Press
Publisher: Peter Norton
Associate Publisher: Ana Parker
Art Director: Charles McStravick
Acquisitions Editor: Kathryn Chipinka Dalby
Editor: Angela Garcia

Produced by OH!
Publisher: Kate Pollard
Editor: Susan Clark
Author: Jason Ward
Art direction and illustration: Evi-O.Studio | Kait Polkinghorne

Library of Congress Control Number: 2021932471

ISBN: 978-1-64517-590-2

Printed in Dubai

25 24 23 22 21 1 2 3 4 5